Becoming:
A Spiritual Journey

Rev. Pamela A Feeser

For Duffy

God wishes to be known; and it pleases him that we should rest in him; for
everything which is beneath him is not sufficient for us.

Julian of Norwich
Showings

CONTENTS

ACKNOWLEDGMENTS

Thank you to C. E. Ré Robbins of Tavernier, Florida, for not only creating the stunning painting on the cover but also for allowing me to use it on the cover of my book, again. The painting's title is Childhood's End.

I first saw the painting at a fund-raiser in the Upper Keys of Florida. From my first glance, it has had a breathtaking effect on me with its amazing expression of the dynamic and continual relationship between the Triune God and humanity. I see the brilliant circular light as the Light of God, the birth canal as the Creator, the flames as the Holy Spirit, the children and woman as humanity, and the movement of the painting through and around the spiral of life and life-giving divinity as the ongoing relationship between humanity and the divine. I see spirituality.

Ré Robbins was touched by my interpretation of her painting and gave me permission to use it as my book cover. Her work can be found at www.art4spirit.com.

I don't know what I would have done without the support, encouragement, advice, and patience of my loving husband, Delbert Carter, and my colleague, Dr. Teddy Tarr. Thank you for your words, time, suggestions, and mostly love while helping me to finish my book. I love you both. May you always know God's blessings through all things.

Pam .

The introduction provides a brief opening to the idea of spirituality and how it relates to daily living as well as religion. The first chapter starts with the beginning of my spiritual life and explores beginnings. Your beginning will not be the same as mine. However, it will be or was just as special and unique. From there I take a look at how I worked through those beginnings into chapter two. In this chapter I invite you, the reader, to join me on a spiritual journey from a common foundation, each of us claiming our brokenness and moving forward from that place. We begin from where we are, and that's okay. If we start from where we aren't, if we pretend we are more whole than we are, our relationship will not be true. Something will be missing until we are honest with, at least, ourselves. Chapter three invites introspection, encouraging you, once again, to be honest with yourself. You will be invited to laugh with me over my flaws and celebrate the amazing joy of self-discovery and healing that takes place when we share grace with ourselves. Chapter four will encourage you to reach out to others, the world, and creation, delighting in the miraculous gifts to your living in the process. Chapter five invites you to rummage through the many lessons I've learned as I've searched myself, gaining the courage and strength to represent who I truly am through my living. In other words, the fidelity of moral maturation is explored through true-life successes and struggles. Chapter six is my way of expressing that wonderful African adage: when the toe is stubbed, the eye cries. Chapter seven addresses morality. How do we develop our morality? How do we develop our moral stance? Chapter eight delves into our relating with a higher power. My higher power is often referred to by others as the Triune God. If I had to choose one way of referring to the one who loved me into being perhaps I would use Creator. This is simply because the place where my life and this One seem to resonate the most beautifully is concerning creativity, creation, humor, life, expression. Finally, chapter nine is a springboard into continuing the process.

INTRODUCTION

Life is the most complex and challenging thing you will ever do. Some people choose to skate along the surface, while others choose to live. Each person has his or her own reasons for making choices about how to deal with life. Fear, arrogance, faith, personal identity … there are numerous things that influence who you are and who you choose to be. I remember struggling with the age-old question of nurture versus nature when I was in high school psychology class. Life was so "seemingly" simple back then. However, even then my belief was that it is both nature and nurture. My belief was based on the fact that while my four brothers and I each have our own unique personality, we also share certain characteristics. Duffy was born one year ahead of me. Then I have three younger brothers who are seven, ten, and thirteen years younger. We grew up in the same household with the same parents but in two separate groups as a result of our age differences and a terrible accident that took my older brother's life before the three younger ones were born. As the years continued, I gained more experience, knowledge, and influence of all sorts. Now I am absolutely convinced that life is all inclusive. I believe that there are certain characteristics that seem to be a part of us from the time we are born. I believe this is most evident in twins. At the same time, life does not discriminate. Everything the individual is subjected to, whether it is experienced willingly or unwillingly, is taken in by that person's life, by their being.

How we deal with, process, and utilize life experiences is a matter of our spirituality. In the twenty-first century, many people are becoming more and more interested in spirituality. At the same time, there are many who feel threatened by it. Spirituality is actually as natural to us as breathing. Unfortunately, humanity has pushed spirituality aside for hundreds if not thousands of years in interest of structured beliefs. Additionally, systematic ways of living have been prescribed based on those beliefs. Yes, I'm talking about organized religion. Organized religion and spirituality are not intended to be mutually exclusive. However, in the interest of religious fidelity, spirituality has often been pushed aside as being too harshly judged and regulated. The balance between the two has become drastically out of balance. Religion is intended to give guidance to our spiritual lives, among other things. It is not intended to dictate our beliefs or stop us from thinking for ourselves. Spirituality is intended to be the way we grow in our relationship with that which is greater than ourselves. It is not intended to replace religion.

As a United Methodist pastor, I have discovered an incredible wealth of spirituality among those the Church so often labels the "lost." Rather than finding people outside the traditional church to be spiritless, lost, and empty, I've found many of them to be asking wonderfully deep, significant questions while seeking relationship with the divine grace. Unfortunately, these are questions that I often do not hear people in the pews asking. Religion, just like spirituality, has its dangers and its great gifts.

Throughout my life, I've had many experiences, and when it comes down to it, my spirituality is what has literally kept me alive. Spirituality is a living, life-giving, divine gift. Again, I stress that my church, my religion, has been an important source of structure, guidance, and fellowship in my life of faith. It's not a question of either/or; rather, for me, it needs to be both/and.

I pray that this book may be inspirational to you in your living. I pray that you might come to truly love yourself even more and more purely as you come to love and relate with the whole of being. I pray for blessings on you and yours.

Lover of my very being, you have so enriched and blessed and nurtured and held and consoled and challenged and embraced every cell of my brokenness. You have led me to wholeness and love and grace and blessedness and yes, always to you. And now you call me to this which I offer back to you for even more blessings that these stories and thoughts might stir others and me to know you and be known by you more deeply and more completely than ever before. You know that I've done the very best I can. May your graciousness take this offering and give it light and life.

Shalom
Pam

CHAPTER ONE : BEGINNINGS

O God, you are my God,
I seek you, my soul thirsts for you;
my flesh faints for you,
as in a dry and weary land where there is no water.
So I have looked upon you in the sanctuary,
beholding your power and glory.
Because your steadfast love is better than life,
my lips will praise you.
So I will bless you as long as I live;
I will lift up my hands and call on your name.
My soul is satisfied as with a rich feast,
and my mouth praises you with joyful lips
when I think of you on my bed,
and meditate on you in the watches of the night;
for you have been my help,
and in the shadow of your wings I sing for joy.
My soul clings to you;
your right hand upholds me.

Psalm 63:1¬8

Excitement and pride swelled in my heart. It was coming, finally the long-awaited first day of school. Even better, I was going to be a first grader, with my big brother and best friend, Duffy in the second grade—right there for me whenever I needed him. That day couldn't come fast enough.

However, the weekend before school was to begin, our family was in a violent accident involving a Mack truck. Duffy died. I remember asking to see my brother while I was in the hospital. They kept telling me he was in surgery, and this made me frustrated and angry. Then the day came that we were going home; finally, I could see my brother. I was excited. Mom, Dad, Aunt Jackie, Grampa, and I got into the car. As the car pulled away from the hospital, I shouted, "Wait! We can't forget Duffy!" There was silence, dead silence, as the car pulled away. When we arrived home, Mom and Dad called me over and told me that Duffy had died. "No!" I accused them of lying. Duffy couldn't be dead. But … I knew it was true.

During the following months, family, the pastor, and friends would come to visit. They would walk right by me and go into the room with Mom and Dad. They were in the room where I wasn't allowed to be. I wanted and needed to talk, to be held and comforted, to be told that I was loved, but I did not know how to ask for this and did not perceive it being offered.

When my injuries had healed to the point that I could go outside to play again, the first place I went was a few houses down the road to the church. I knew God was there, and more important, I knew God would listen. I silently opened the door and tiptoed in. Children were not allowed to be in the church by themselves. I could hear the sexton's son vacuuming the basement floor. I could see the sexton, his mother, preparing the Communion table. Behind the last pew, in the corner, there was a table where I could hide. The worst thing that could happen was to be discovered and told to leave. I silently slipped under the table, leaned against the wall, looked into the colored light coming through the stained glass window, and cried my heart out to God. I'm not quite sure how to describe the feeling of those moments. It was like nothing else existed but God and me. I gave God all my anger, frustration, confusion, and pain. I placed it all on God. We cried, talked, and held each other. While I was clinging to God, I remember feeling like God was holding me close in the cup of his great big hand. I looked around me for God's hand. That hand wasn't physical, but it was real. God loved me, and nothing was more important.

So many times in life we wish we could feel the love of our higher power, our God, the Divine, our Creator, Allah, Yahweh, or some transcendent other. But we just can't. Sometimes the holier-than-thou attitude of so-called Christians has turned us off. We wonder what is wrong with us or them or both. In defense, sometimes we decide that there is no higher power or no higher power we want to have anything to do with; we are on our own. We struggle through these dark tunnels in our lives, wandering lost through the dry desert, becoming increasingly convinced we are alone. Yet, there are signs, if only we can recognize them. Maybe a friend reaching out without being asked, a stranger with a smile, someone worse off than ourselves sharing encouraging words, the beauty of creation resonating deep in our souls, stirring life in heartwarming ways. There are many ways we can begin to recognize that which is greater than ourselves.

There is a balm in Gilead
To make the wounded whole;
There is a balm in Gilead
To heal the sin sick soul.
Sometimes I feel discouraged,
And think my work's in vain,
But then the Holy Spirit
Revives my soul again.

African-American spiritual

Recognition is a choice, our choice. We begin by searching for the true source of the goodness, however obscured by the brokenness of our lives and living. Recognizing takes courage. We can easily talk ourselves out of our search and back into the desert. Believing in something intangible takes confidence in oneself. Sometimes confidence comes as a result of childlike faith; sometimes it comes out of desperation. Wherever the confidence comes from, it gives us the strength to consider something we hadn't been willing to or able to consider before.

I was fortunate to have grown up in the Pennsylvania Dutch community. Being surrounded by my wonderful faith environment undergirded me with a foundation that I was able to draw upon when I needed it the most. In the midst of my grief and confusion, these people empowered me to draw on their teachings. I sat on their tattered yet mystical couch receiving the balm of Gilead. However, what I had previously learned only became real when I reached out in trust that day in the sanctuary. The trust wasn't pretty or neat or well-articulated. The trust came out in anger and demands. I demanded that God explain to me what he could possibly have been thinking to take my brother so young and so violently. I gave God my hate, frustration, and anger. I trusted God to deal with my honest feelings, and God responded.

As I sat under the table crying my heart to God, I suddenly became aware that God was holding me in the palm of his great big hand. This hand was more real than tangibility could prove. I felt God's tears pour down over me, baptizing me with divine life-giving love. Then the wonderful smell of the freshly poured grape juice and freshly cut bread, the elements of Communion, filled my soul in a way that sparked recognition deep inside; recognition of fulfilling life that would take a lifetime for me to bring to fruition. Of course, at six years old, all I knew was that God loved me and nothing was more important. The Church—religion—gave me the foundation to begin this journey. Spirituality deepened and developed my personal relationship with my Creator. This was the beginning of my spiritual living.

□ .

CHAPTER TWO : SPIRITUAL LIVING, SPIRITUALITY

What comes to your mind when you hear the words spirituality or spiritual? Mystic, psychic, pious, saintly, holy, religious, otherworldly, something untouchable, something foreign …?

What feelings swell up inside you? Fear, bewilderment, nervousness, lostness, desire, hope …?

What thoughts fill your mind? *Ugh! This is too far out there. I just don't get it. I want it, but what is it?*

The very first people to walk the earth discovered and celebrated spirituality long before religion was even a thought. As they took those first steps into the world, curiosity gripped them: *What is this, and what does it mean to me?* As they sought to discover who they were in relationship to others, that slithery thing on the ground, those colorful juicy things growing on the vine, that wet pool of blueness with slimy, wiggly things moving around inside it … as they sought to discover and determine their relationship to these things, they discovered and celebrated spirituality. As they wondered about the rain, and lightning, and snow, and thunder, and where it all comes from, they discovered and celebrated spirituality. As they discovered love and joy and fear and loneliness and questioned why, how, and what possible meaning these feelings could have for them, they discovered spirituality. As they began to formulate opinions and struggle with differences, they began the entry into spiritual living. When they called out to whomever or whatever was out there that early people knew was greater than themselves, they began living as spiritual beings.

Yet today, after the passing of many eras and amazing developments in, by, and through people, even today spirituality holds a certain mystique for us. With this mystique comes a fear of what the unknown might do to us, yet a desire to know the mysterious. The truth is that spirituality is as natural and basic to each of us as it was to those first people. The truth is also that spirituality and religion are not necessarily mutually exclusive. Many people choose to live spiritual lives only. I believe this is possible, but without a foundation from which to exercise discernment, a person can end up believing in everything—thus nothing. Many people try to live religious but not spiritual lives. I don't believe this is possible if a religious person truly follows the tenets of their religion. Religion is a set of rules, rituals, and beliefs that a community of people chooses to follow that leads them to live in accordance with their God or gods. In short, religion is a tool to develop our spirituality. To practice a religion as nothing more than a set of dos and don'ts and rituals to enjoy among your community of like-minded friends is to reduce religion to a useless, albeit self-satisfying, pastime. I am a spiritual Christian.

Spirituality begins within us. Spirituality begins when we look deeper. I hope to share my journey in a way that helps you along yours. For years, friends and colleagues have asked me over and over again to write a book. "You have been through so much and not only survived but thrived. Others need to hear your story to help them through their crisis." It's true that I have been through some incredible experiences. The way that I've chosen to work through and interpret my experiences has been guided by what I have come to call the "somehow" of my life. Most people will recognize this "somehow" as my beloved companion, the Holy Spirit.

One of my earliest significant experiences happened when I was six years old. The sanctuary story above is from that time. My family struggled through the following years, each of us trying to make sense of what happened in ways that pulled us apart. My father became a very difficult person to live with. Even so, he continued to provide for us with his strong work ethic. My mother had three more children after the accident, and her focus was on the family. I turned to God, music, and education. I was very angry and alone for many years. We each struggled through our own journeys. It would be many years before we found one another again.

Throughout the process, there were a number of significant turning points in my life. Somehow I chose to use each one of these experiences to grow spiritually. It would be many years before I understood what that "somehow" was. Yet, through it all I was aware of its presence. I just didn't know what it was. In the pages to follow, I'll share some of these experiences with you, and my struggles through them. My words and my experiences certainly are not the final word. They are simply a sharing from me to you.

Your experiences will not be the same, but whatever your experiences are, you also have the power to choose how you will use them. It's not too late. I pray that if my offerings resonate with your life, you might be encouraged. You might begin to recognize the divine healing embrace around you. Then may you allow that creative energy of the Divine help you cultivate a life and way of living out of all that has brought you there.

We need a common starting point to begin our journey together. Let's allow that starting point to be a definition of what we seek: spirituality. There are as many definitions for this essential to life as there are people. In their book *The Spirituality of Imperfection: Storytelling and the Journey to Wholeness*, Kurtz and Ketcham wisely pull examples from interfaith resources throughout history. Introducing the idea of spirituality, they quote Lao Tzu: "Those who know do not say; those who say do not know."[1] The point is that spirituality is intangible, greater than words, and therefore difficult to describe. While I respect your right and responsibility to develop your own definition, for the purposes of this exploration I invite you to use my working definition as I share my journey with you. My life experiences,

---

[1] Ernest Kurtz and Katherine Ketcham, *The Spirituality of Imperfection: Storytelling and the Journey to Wholeness* (New York: Bantam Books, 1992), 15.

research, relationships, and personal exploration have all contributed to the formation of this definition. If you don't already have one, I hope you will begin to develop your own definition throughout the course of our journey together. At the same time, please remember that any definition of spirituality must be a work in progress. That is, there is always more for us to discover. Any definition of spirituality is simply our best effort to express that which we've discovered and experienced to date.

My definition of spirituality:

The dynamic process of developing one's depth of being through introspection, reaching out, developing a relational expansion of worldview, moral maturation, and intentional living, all within the context of a personal relationship with a higher power. For any person to truly live life fully, spirituality is essential.

Every experience of our living has potential to lead us to or away from our spiritual center, the Divine with whom we relate. The choice is ours to claim; however, life sometimes surrounds this choice with a thick fog making it hard to find our way through. The various aspects of the spiritual process can be taken in any order. This lifelong process is holistic and ever present. If any aspect of the process is skipped, we suffer spiritually.

When we decide to run the Boston Marathon, we don't just get up and run it. Rather, we begin with small steps first, conditioning our bodies bit by bit. In the same way, we begin our spiritual journey with small steps. We begin by reflecting on what has brought us to the point of desiring a spiritual journey. Whatever it was that led us to this point is our stepping-stone. Wherever we are now is our starting point, because this is where spirituality first resonated within our being. The music begins.

The word *spirituality* comes from the Latin word *spiritus* meaning "breath" in the sense of breath of life. The Greek word is πνευμα (pneuma) or πνευματικωσ (pneumatikos) meaning "inner life, spirit, disposition, state of mind, wind, breath." So, take a deep breath and slowly let it out. Do it again and think about the breath of life, that which enlivens your very being. Did you ever think about where that breath comes from … the source of all being? It's okay that you don't have a definition for that source. The source knows itself and will reveal itself as you grow as the spiritual being you are. In fact, the spiritual journey is a lifelong journey of discovery, continually gaining a deeper understanding of life and living and being. The difficulty is all the muck of life that we think distracts us from our journey. However, it is precisely these distractions that help us define our spiritual selves. It's not always easy to figure out which way to go when we are just focusing on the fires of life. Rather, it is when we are working through those fires, keeping our focus on that which is greater even in the midst of chaos that we are able to continue on our journey.

After I graduated from college with a BS in Music Education, I just knew that I would get to teach wonderfully hungry children to express themselves through the mystery of music. I was trained and licensed as a band director and eager to share the joy of music I'd known throughout my life. My life was planned out. As the band director of a school, I would begin to build the program. Students would come to me for private lessons. We would have a competing marching band, a concert band, a jazz band. The students would be excited to learn about the composers and would develop their expression, interpretation, and understanding of music. This would take several years to build, but that was perfect. I would get involved in the community theater and the music ministry at church. Then I would begin to look for someone to share my wonderful life with. He would have established himself and we would be deeply in love. Maybe we would have a child. We would buy a house and build a life together. Oh what a wonderful life I was going to have.

Ah yes, it's always important to dream. Music is the heart of my soul; and sharing its wonders with children who give life to creativity with their every breath was exciting. However, first I had to get a teaching job. One school wouldn't even interview me because women were not considered appropriate band directors. Another school granted me the interview; however, they informed me that I was too short and small to command the respect of high school kids. Another school hired me and gave excellent evaluations twice in my first year. The third evaluation of that same year was so poor that I was given two weeks to leave. I still have no idea what I did that was so terrible. I was so devastated and horrified, young and inexperienced that I just left with my head down. My music ministry at the church also was not going so well. Confusion reigned in my chaotic world. I was stunned; the heart of my soul, the life-giving gift God gave me, and I was suddenly a total failure at sharing it. How could this be? I took a break and fell back on my secondary training: bookkeeping. Meanwhile I did find love, and we chose to marry and build a life together.

If we continue to be distracted by letting the fires of life burn us out, we become more and more empty, looking for something to fill us up. Stress can come from anywhere, and each person reacts to stress in different ways. Some people turn to things that provide a numbing sense such as alcohol or drugs just to mask the overwhelming fear or frustration. These things that do not directly address the issue only serve to empty us and disempower us all that much more. Our lives become hollow and dry.

One of my favorite stories is about the valley of dry bones found in Ezekiel 37:1–14.

There was an average Hebrew man named Ezekiel living in what we now know as the Middle East. He lived about 2,900 years ago, during the time that his people were captured by the Babylonians after destroying Jerusalem. He was born into a priestly family, which is significant in Hebraic heritage. This required him to serve as a priest to his people throughout his life, even throughout the Babylonian Diaspora.[2]

While his people struggled under siege, Ezekiel had many experiences with YHWH (pronounced Yahweh, "the God of the Hebrews"). YHWH promises to deliver the house of Israel and bring them into their own land once again. How powerful this promise must have sounded to Ezekiel. Can you imagine having your home,

---

[2] James L. Mays and Patrick D. Miller, eds., *Interpretation: A Bible Commentary for Teaching and Preaching.* Blenkinsopp, Joseph. Vol. Ezekiel. (Louisville, KY: John Knox Press, 1990), 8.

community, culture, and country destroyed, and then you are taken to the land of the people who committed this atrocity? Then, if that wasn't enough, imagine being forced to live in a culture not your own, one that contradicts your own ethics and beliefs, and surrounded by people speaking a language not your own—exile. Imagine losing contact with the people you grew up with and depended on for community. Imagine this continuing for approximately thirty years. I can understand how the Jews felt abandoned by YHWH. Can you? Have you felt abandoned, exiled?

I can only imagine the enormity of the task God set before Ezekiel. One day God took Ezekiel and placed him in the middle of a valley full of the bones of the slain. Now these weren't just a few bones, but they literally filled the valley. Piles of bones on bones, and God's Spirit (*ruah* meaning spirit, breath, or wind) carried Ezekiel through and all around for miles. These were old dry bones. Bones that had been exposed for a very long time with no life left in them. God asked Ezekiel, "Mortal, can these bones live?" (v. 3). Can you imagine the depth of pain in Ezekiel's heart? Can you imagine his disbelief over the question, "Can these bones live?" Are you kidding!

What are these dry bones in your life? For me they often represent the dry bones of the domestic violence in our society.

I stood with Ezekiel in the middle of the valley of dry bones confounded by the divine question, "Mortal, can these bones live?" We looked around; the divine wind led us all over the valley deep with dry bones.

I went to my pastor for help. I told him how [Ralph] was beating me. My pastor asked me, "What are you doing to make him so angry?"—A victim.

I'm so scared! He's going to kill us! The last time I asked him to leave he started up the drill and told me he was going to sink the houseboat [where they lived]. He badgers my twelve-year-old son mercilessly for hours. Finally, [my son] gets so frustrated he slams his fist into the wall. I talked with the guidance counselor at school. She is going to enroll him [her son] in anger management classes.—A victim.

There's no domestic violence in my congregation.—A pastor.

I'm tired of going in and rescuing her when all she does is turns right around and goes back. She's just asking for it.—A deputy sheriff.

No, we are not interested in offering domestic violence training in our seminary.—President of a seminary.

Pam, you must stop talking about such things [domestic violence] in your sermons. We are not up there to air our dirty laundry.—A retired clergyperson.

We don't know that domestic violence is going on in our neighbor's house unless we become Peeping Toms. It's none of our business. It has nothing to do with us.—A friend.

The church is the only place where some people get to be leaders. So, we must allow anyone who volunteers and has the desire to lead to take the position. We don't have enough volunteers as it is.—A mentoring clergyperson.

I can't tell my boss! If he knew my husband was stalking me and threatening to kill me, I'd be fired!—A coworker.[3]

Yet, this is God, YHWH, the *ruah,* the divine Spirit. How would you respond? After consideration, my friend Ezekiel says, "Oh God, you know" (v. 3). What else could he say? This is God he is responding to. Of course God knows. In fact, Ezekiel can't even begin to imagine how they could possibly live. For goodness sake, he can envision plenty of walking, talking, breathing people who are not alive, and God wants to know if these dead, hollow, dry bones can live. Sure God, anything you say. Who am I to question you?

Then, if he hadn't already experienced enough, Ezekiel receives a divine command. "Prophesy to these bones, and say to them: O dry bones, hear the word of the Lord. Thus says the Lord God to these bones: I will cause flesh to come upon you, and cover you with skin, and put breath in you, and you shall live; and you shall know that I

---

[3]The Rev. Pamela Feeser, D. Min. *Buying the Vineyard: Different Options for Living, Playing, and Hoping in Non-violence and Safety: DOLPHINS.* Miami, FL: Dissertation for doctoral work at South Florida Center for Theological Studies, 2003.

am the Lord" (v. 6).

WOW! What would you do? You've not only seen, but also lived with and among the dead, dry bones surrounding you. You know their power. You know the devastation. "Prophesy," God says to you. Prophesy. Wouldn't it be so easy to just tuck tail and run the other way? Hide in a bottle or a pill or anything to not have to be aware of the touch of this parched complete death. Hide behind your anger, your disempowerment, anything. But the *ruah* calls, the Spirit carries, God commands, "Prophesy, mortal, prophesy."

So Ezekiel prophesied. It couldn't have been easy. Would they hear? Why, why this time when never before? And there is a rattling as the bones came together. But, these bones are turning to dust; how can they possibly live? In stunned amazement, Ezekiel looked on and there were sinews on them and flesh had come upon them, and skin had covered them; but … there was no breath in them. So stunning a display before him, he looked on with bewilderment. Here he was with breath and life and a person of faith, and he doubted. Yet, these dead, dry, powdered bones responded. How could it be possible?

Now, God said to him, "Prophesy to the breath, prophesy, mortal, and say to the breath; Thus says the Lord God: Come from the four winds, o breath, and breathe upon these slain, that they may live" (v. 9).

Ezekiel prophesied and just as God said, breath came into them and they lived and stood on their feet (vv. 1–14).

While my dream of teaching music through the public school system didn't pan out, God had something much greater in store for me. My music has become a significant part of my ministry. Music informs my way of thinking, my way of perceiving, as well as my communication style. Music also has proven a powerful tool for sharing God's message both in obvious and not so obvious ways. Many times music has also paved the way for my ministry almost always surprising myself as well as others. When I focused only on the short-term fire, I thought I was a failure. However, as I have continued to focus on God's presence and calling on my life, a beautiful blossom has developed.

Are you ready? The dry bones can live. But, there is a process, a process of growth with the *ruah*, the Spirit. It won't all happen at once, just as with the bones in the valley, there were steps, one at a time. Take a breath. Let it out and breathe in again, deeper this time. Envision your bones, your dry bones, breathe in the *ruah* and blow it out over your bones. We begin our journey of a lifetime.

Activity 1

1. What is your understanding of spirituality? What is the difference between spirituality and religion?

2. Review my definition of spirituality: the dynamic process of developing one's depth of being through introspection, reaching out, developing a relational expansion of worldview, moral maturation, and intentional living, all within the context of personal relationship with a higher power. For any person to truly live life fully, spirituality is essential. Is this a definition of spirituality that you feel you can work with through your reading of this book? If not, take note of the changes you need to make to the definition and why. As you read the rest of the book, keep these changes in mind as you progress in your reading.

3. Write down anything that jumps out at you in this chapter and each succeeding chapter.

CHAPTER THREE : INTROSPECTION

Who are you? Who are you really? What do you stand for? What do you believe?

Being honest with ourselves about who we are, about our state of being, is one of the most difficult things for most of us to do. Well, it is for me anyway. The reflections of others on who we are can help guide our search for self, but others will never know the depths within us. The truth of our being can only ever truly be known by ourselves and the one who loved us into being, our Creator, Higher Power, Lover, Mother, Father, God, Redeemer, Holy Spirit, Source of All Being.

While I have been introspective most of my adult life, I must admit that I can be very good at rationalizing, justifying, and denying my flaws and even my strengths. I didn't even realize that I'm a perfectionist until a year ago! I thought, How can I be a perfectionist? I'm forever messing up. And yes, I do chuckle about this.

We tend to have issues with imperfection or even the perception of imperfection. We wash our dishes before putting them into the dishwasher. We clean the house before the cleaning service comes. We are embarrassed if we don't know the answer. We tend to interpret strength as being in control of self, others, and our environment (or at least the impression of control). We tend to interpret strength as not showing strong emotions. We even judge people whose physical or mental strengths are different than what we consider "normal" to be handicapped rather than normal themselves. We feel sorry for or judgmental of anyone who is not "normal." Then, if something happens to us that makes us "not normal" such as losing a leg or the ability to hear, our psyche goes into a roller-coaster ride searching for our identity.

When I was in my early forties, five months after getting married, my new husband and I were riding a train when it derailed. My injuries, both physical and emotional, were extensive, and many were permanent. I had even lost my life in the aftermath. Adding to my losses, my husband, who fortunately had only sustained emotional injuries, left me shortly after the accident. He told me he didn't want an injured wife; he didn't want to have to take care of me.

My psychologist has been a significant resource during my healing. The following conversation was part of one of our early sessions.

She said, "You're not the same person you were when you entered the train."

"Yes I am!" I desperately shouted back.

"No Pam, the person who walked onto that train is gone. You are not the same person," my psychologist responded.

I shuddered with rage and disbelief. I couldn't let go of the person I was before. Prior to the train wreck, I had worked so hard to learn to love myself, to work on my growing edges, claim my gifts, heal my wounds, and move forward. Life had never been easy, but I'd always faced it head-on. I had come so far. I had been so happy. I wasn't perfect. Life wasn't perfect. But, I was happy and loved facing my challenges.

A challenge … this train wreck was not a challenge. It was a monster, a life-eating, hope-killing, evil-permeating monster of the most hideous kind. It had taken everything—my husband, my home, my marriage, my music, my career, my body, my very life, my ability to think, my strength, my health, everything. And now, to give in and accept that it took even me, my being, the person I had come to be and love; this was just too much. No! I put my foot down. No! I could not be that pathetic. I refused to give what remained of my identity to the train too. No!

Looking back to that unspeakably painful time, I now realize that at the time I couldn't imagine how I could ever come back to living life. It was too much. How does one heal after losing so much? How would it be possible? Without even having me to begin the process, who or what did I have?

Think back to the times in your life when you felt you just couldn't continue on. Life was too hard. Maybe you felt alone, betrayed, abandoned, or angry, powerless, frustrated. What happened that led you to that place in your life? Maybe there's some shame or guilt involved. It's okay to acknowledge those terrible feelings and claim them.

There's nothing wrong with feelings regardless of the reasons behind them. What's wrong is when we bottle them up and deny them. The emotions we feel are there for a reason. They tell us something is either wrong or right. Our feelings don't betray us; we betray them. The danger comes when we ignore, push away, or deny our true feelings. How we respond to our feelings and with our feelings is very important. What we do with our feelings or as a result of our feelings is also very important.

So, what did you do with your feelings during and after this difficult time? Did you resolve them in a healthy, life-giving way? Or did you stuff them? If they were stuffed, you can be assured that they still are and will strike back at a most inopportune moment. So, who or what do you have to help you resolve this?

The authors of The Spirituality of Imperfection give us these words of hope:

"God comes through the wound: Our very imperfections—what

religions label our sins, what therapy calls our sickness, what philosophy terms our errors—are precisely what bring us closer to the reality that no matter how hard we try to deny it, we are not the one in control here. And this realization, inevitably and joyously, brings us closer to 'God':

One of the disconcerting—and delightful—teachings of the master was: "God is closer to sinners than to saints."

This is how he explained it: "God in heaven holds each person by a string. When you sin, you cut the string, and then God ties it up again, making a knot—and thereby bringing you a little closer to him. Again and again your sins cut the string—and with each further knot God keeps drawing you closer and closer.'"

What did I have? I had the only thing besides my dog that I didn't lose. I had my deep abiding relationship with God, the one who held me and claimed me with baptismal tears that day under the table so many years ago. That same day, I had also claimed my responsibility for my relationship with my Creator, the divine holiness, my God.

Spirituality is claiming our flaws along with those things about ourselves we are proud of and loving our complete selves. We tend to think that the things we are proud of are our strengths. However, it is the claim of and acceptance of the dichotomies within us that is our strength. Then having the courage and strength to place our newly claimed and accepted self at the feet of the one who loved us into being, this is spirituality.

When we acknowledge our flaws, it is so easy to beat ourselves up. I've always found this phenomenon amazing. If we really think about it … what good does that do anyone? Yet, more often than not, there we are being our worst enemy when we're down. For many years, I unknowingly struggled with my perfectionism. My expectations of myself have always been outrageously high. Most of my life I was in denial that I am a perfectionist when focused on myself. Oddly enough, I have amazing patience, grace, and forgiveness for others. As long as someone is trying to do their best and the right thing, I am very happy to celebrate with them, to work with them, and to encourage them. Sharing that same life-giving space with myself has been a very difficult thing for me to learn. The patriarchal interpretation is that I think more highly of myself than I do of others. Therefore, I expect myself to do better, achieve more. This might be the tendency for men, I don't know. However, it is not the truth for me. My judgmental perfectionism is not about me comparing myself with others; it's about not having a good relationship with myself.

Of course, I could go back to a Freudian review of this, but I don't find that helpful. Rather, I find life through a Systems approach. In Family Systems, rather than going back to our childhood, the idea is to look at and redefine our relationships and roles in the here and now to effect changes that can help us heal. This approach was first developed by Murray Bowen. Rabbi Edwin Friedman, in his book Generation to Generation: Family Process in Church and Synagogue, applied Bowen's Theory to institutional as well as to person-to-person relationships within a faith-based framework. By looking at the here and now, I've been able to redefine my role in the fellowship of life, the body of Christ, the cloud of witnesses. My understanding of God's love for me has been the core of my being since I was six years old. However, I needed to move that "understanding" to deeply claiming. Claiming this life-giving divine love for the whole of me, not just in my core, but in each of my cells. This was the growth I needed to make.

Cellular woundedness is something I became aware of following the train wreck. Previously, I had no idea this could even happen. Cellular woundedness is most often heard of with PTSD (post-traumatic stress disorder). I now live with chronic PTSD as well as RSD (reflex sympathetic dystrophy) as a result of the combination of PTSD, severe trauma, and nerve damage over most of my body. However, the trauma that I experienced, that my body experienced, was so complete and so violent and the length of time that these wounds happened over and over again was so long (two years), healing was no longer a matter of mere therapies and curing became impossible. Healing became about learning to deeply embrace myself with life-giving gracious loving that only comes from one's relationship with the one who will never walk away.

In order to choose to heal, I had to choose to live. While I had clearly fought alongside the medical professionals to bring me, literally, back to life, I was slowly dying during these painful years of struggling to heal. My injuries were so complete, everyone would have allowed me to use them as an excuse to stop living. I could very easily have chosen to go on SSI, retire on disability, and just be miserable for the rest of my "life." No one would have questioned it. Now I think back and ask myself why did I choose to live?

Note: Following the train wreck, I was diagnosed with chronic PTSD. J. LeBron McBride, PhD wrote a wonderfully sensitive and well-researched book called Spiritual Crisis: Surviving Trauma to the Soul. While I fully agree with McBride that chronic PTSD can often lead to alienation from God and a lost sense of hope, gratefully I am able to assure readers that this is not always the case. In fact, it was my close relationship and trust in God that has kept me alive throughout this horrid ordeal. However, even with strength of soul, there have been definite spiritual wounds that have needed my attention and divine healing. For me, the woundedness of my soul was directed toward other people, religion, denominationalism, security, institutions, and trust of a number of things, all of which, of course, affects my relationship with God. This woundedness will be addressed further in some of the following sections.

On December 13, 2004, a year and a half after the train wreck, I wrote down a few thoughts:

What are my hopes and dreams for the future? What do I want to be? What do I want to contribute? All these questions are related to: Who am I? But it's also more than that.

In the past, creating myself was always exciting. A wonderful blank slate that I could put anything on that I wanted. And the me that I created and was creating was one that I truly loved. What a fulfilling experience that was. There was a time that I didn't love myself, but I worked through all that. Now I had fallen in love with me and treasured the gifts I had to offer and offered them to the world, my local and extended communities without reserve. When others rejected me of course it hurt some, but it didn't damage me. Because I had fully accepted and fallen in love with who I was and was becoming. I had built a great reputation as a musician, teacher, spiritual leader, and domestic violence consultant. I was respected in all those roles and in many communities.

Then the train wreck wrecked it all. It just destroyed everything. Broke into bits what it didn't completely destroy. Totally and completely devastated, I am now charged with the responsibility of rebuilding me, my life, my purpose, and my sense of value and worth. It's like falling deeply in love and then after years of dedication to the relationship having it blow up in your face and trying to learn to love again. But it's even worse. Because it's not just one aspect of my life and me—it's the whole thing.

It's not that I don't want to. I ache to. It's how do I gather up the courage? The courage to rebuild, to recreate, to love, to truly love me again and the whole time knowing (and expecting) that it will all be blown to bits yet again. ... How do I re-create the courage that can withstand another hit like this one, again?

I keep thinking about Jeremiah. That astonishing text that has held me, challenged me, and encouraged me since Christmas of two years ago: Jeremiah 32.

Jerusalem had become a city of apathy, a city overrun by hopelessness. The fields are dead, wells are dry, and their enemy, Babylon, is about to overtake them. They have given up and have no fight left in them. Jeremiah, deeply pained by the state of God's people, warns them of doom at the hands of the Chaldeans. His friend, King Zedekiah, interprets his words as words of betrayal and puts him in jail. In the midst of his muck, God tells Jeremiah to go buy the vineyard of his cousin who could no longer afford it. Imagine how ludicrous this seemed. All was lost. Who in their right mind would go buy dead land that was about to be taken by enemies? What kind of an investment is that?

Jeremiah's eyes are opened. This is an investment of hope. Yes, the people have turned away, but they will turn back. God will not abandon them; in fact, God will make an everlasting covenant with them to always and in all things work for the good. Yes, buy the vineyard. Plant seeds of hope and nurture those seeds even when buried with muck. Do the hard work, look for the good, water with love, and spend the time. We must invest to bring hope to life. Vineyards will be bought and sold again. Fortunes will be restored. But, first we buy the vineyard.

It was two years ago that I chose to, again, buy the vineyard. I had no idea that the muck would get so terribly much deeper, but I knew that it might get worse. What is my vineyard? To live again, to choose life, and to rebuild, re-create, to heal. Just as Jeremiah had no idea what fruits his vineyard would bring in the future, nor do I. But I do have faith that it will. And I have been faithful. I have continued against all odds to fight for my healing both physical and now emotional. Unfortunately, healing is not cure and most definitely is not in my case.

The physical battles that I have fought in the past two years have been astounding and seemingly overwhelming most of the time. But I continued to fight. I have come a long, long way. I have been very faithful. My Creator and I have struggled through this whole thing together. We have fought and cried, screamed, bled deeply, and through it all I continue to find myself, again, in the palm of God's great big hand, washed with divine tears and filled with powerful and gentle holy whisperings of the Spirit into my soul.

[my prayer] *God! I hurt; the physical pain is great but nothing compared to my emotional pain. I want so very badly to heal. I continue to do the hard work, to look for the good, to water with love and spend the time. I know this is taking forever, but then you knew it wouldn't be overnight, didn't you? I know I've been saying ugly things to myself about myself. It's not that I really believe them. I'm tired. I'm very, very scared, scared of losing it all, all over again. I'm afraid that I might give up if it happened again. And I don't want to. Others are clueless. They try but can't identify. I'm glad they've never been so completely devastated in this way. I try to help them understand but always to no avail. Bottom line is it's you and me. And I know we can do it. I wish it could be overnight, but then good things, the really really good things always take time. I guess I'm pretty valuable, huh?*

So, on with the battle ...

My loving Creator, help me find the courage: How do I create the courage that can withstand another hit like this one, again? That's so important to me right now. I want to fully live and never give up until I don't have a choice. What tools can I build now that will help me later too?

This snippet of my writing represents the turning point for me. The path did not get any easier afterward. In fact, it became even more difficult because now I had direction and was determined to take action. But, I bought the vineyard. I claimed me. I claimed divine life-giving, healing, all-encompassing love for me, all of the post–train wreck me. I drew the courage and strength to make this claim through my existing relationship with God, and committed myself to do whatever it took to live out this claim. I knew that as long as I was in denial, I couldn't move toward healing. If I didn't move toward healing, I would continue to struggle to live in this same way. I would continue to tread water at best. But with my waning strength I would have drowned. Sometimes, facing those things that hold us back feels like the worst thing and the most impossible thing to do; however, it's the only way to move forward.

One of the things I did was to find an exceptionally skilled psychologist who specializes in grief and loss with whom I had previously built a foundation of respect and trust. She is also a woman of examined faith. I knew that I needed someone with great strength and depth to be able to handle the horrid places I would need to go and to be able to handle my strength. With the gracious, tough, professional, and loving ministry of this lady I was able to go into those places of rage, horror, and violence that had taken up residence deep in my soul. We went there somehow (the Holy Spirit) over and over again and again drawing out this explosive poison little by little and nudging life forward bit by bit. It was exhausting and empowering. It was life affirming. Throughout this whole process, I reexamined my faith drawing on its strengths while deepening and broadening its depth.

Another thing I did was to find a healthy catharsis for my rage and anger. I was able to find this outlet through working out, baking, and my music. Following the train wreck, I had been in physical therapy for three years. My health insurance was incredibly helpful throughout the whole ordeal. However, they felt that three years was enough, so I moved to finding a personal trainer who understood my situation and would work with my doctors and physical therapist to develop an appropriate workout for me.

I found the world's best personal trainer. You'll have to come here to find her. She and I are good friends to this day. She taught me how to not only continue to move forward, but she also helped me build trust in my own abilities. She was tough as nails and unbelievably gracious. She created an environment where I could learn how to strengthen my body and balance through a physical workout. She created an environment of encouragement, support, and trust. She trained me so well that now I am able to work out on my own with confidence.

Baking is a joy that my mother taught me growing up. My specialty is cookies. Each Christmas I would make well over one hundred dozen cookies of about eight–twelve varieties and package them up in tins. Then I would create that year's Christmas Cookie Cookbook with a personal message, all the cookie recipes as well as little snippets of treasured memories about each cookie. Next, I would disperse the tins and cookbooks to fifteen–twenty-five people that I had chosen previously. This process would take one whole month. My practice was to pray over the cookies as I made them and the entire process, keeping each of the chosen recipients in mind. The other day, I reconnected with a friend from several years ago, and she told me that she often thinks of those cookies. I think I'm going to make my cookies again this year.

My music is not just something that I do; it is something that I am. Due to secondary nerve injuries in my face, I had lost the ability to play my instruments. Additionally I have difficulty with my breathing since the train wreck. My flute has been with me since I was eight years old, and there was no way I was going to let the train take my music away. A member of the community had heard of my musical skills and had been searching for a private teacher/coach for her daughter, who was an amazing saxophone player. She didn't care that I couldn't play anymore; she knew I could teach.

I don't know how to express the life and encouragement her undying faith in my skills provided for me. While I taught her daughter how to be a musician rather than just to play an instrument (which she just gobbled up and blossomed into the most beautiful rose), I continued to work at my breathing and figuring out how to get a sound out of my flute and saxophones. My student asked me to teach her flute also. One day during lessons, we were working on her flute embouchure and she asked me to demonstrate. I took her flute, lifted it to my mouth, and played a very airy, but definitely played a scale. We both cried. Today, I continue to work out several times a week; cook and bake for my coworkers, neighbors, and friends; and clearly play my flute. Additionally, I am now able to play one song at a time on my soprano sax and about eight measures on my alto. The future continues.

Spirituality is about claiming our flaws along with those things about ourselves we are proud of and loving our complete selves. We tend to think that the things we are proud of are our strengths. However, it is the claiming and acceptance of the dichotomies within us that is our strength.

ACTIVITY 2

What are your strengths and imperfections? Take a piece of paper and begin to write down your list. Write down the easy things first. Take note if your strengths or your imperfections are the easiest for you to write down. Next, write down the things that you feel most secure about, the thing or things that you can truly depend on. Make sure that whatever you wrote down is healthy. Reflect on: How can the things on your second list help you claim the things on your first list that are the hardest for you to love?

☐

CHAPTER FOUR : REACHING OUT

My first wedding was so exciting to get ready for. We had great fun picking out colors and locations, inviting clergy and musicians, picking flowers, and so much more. Well, okay—I did. I must have tried on fifty wedding gowns and then decided on one of the first ones. (I can hear the men groaning now.) Being a professional musician, the selection of musicians and music was very important to me. My fiancé had a friend of the family who played cello like a dream, and her choices of music were tops. We had met in church where I was the director of music, so that was where we proclaimed our vows to one another and God in the presence of family and friends. My childhood pastor was going to come to our current church to assist the pastor in charge.

Drawing up the guest list was quite an eye-opening experience. I had about sixteen sets of aunts and uncles, more than sixty first cousins, and five members of my immediate family. My fiancé, even with a loose definition of family, had maybe twenty people. Then came the real eye-opener: we sat down to decide on the wedding party. My fiancé had an endless list of possibilities. I had only one person on my list. For the first time, I realized that while I knew many people and was liked by many people, I had no close friends other than the one I went to college with who lived in a different state.

My whole focus to that point was in establishing myself in my music career. I had never even thought about the fact that I had no social life, no girlfriends to go out on the town with, no girlfriends to "discuss" the important topics of the day (like guys). I was in my middle twenties and had no intimate circle of friends. I was actually stunned. Now, looking back, I realize how amazing it was that I actually had the time to develop a relationship with my fiancé. Of course, the reason was because I took the time.

When we're younger, we think we have the world by the tail. Then, as we mature, we discover the opposite is true. Living, truly living, takes lots of intentionality, work, patience, grace, guts, and rarely, but sometimes, a blindfold. Nevertheless, living life is what we make it. It's not good enough to just let life happen. In fact, it's not possible. Just letting life happen is not life; it is a slow painful death. Think of life as a participation sport. In order to participate, each person must, at some point, reach out and get involved.

It was during the planning of our wedding that I decided to reach out and get involved. However, this has been a lifelong endeavor. I had learned, starting when I was six years old, not to trust others. When I was in the hospital asking to see my brother and all the adults lied to me, telling me he was in surgery, I learned not to trust others, especially people in authority. Trust is crucial to healthy living; the foundation of trust development begins in childhood.

In his stages of development, Erik Erickson discusses trust and distrust. While he places this at an earlier stage in life, a recent concept of human development takes Erikson's stages and extends them through Bernes Transactional Analysis. This concept, named Cycles of Development, was coined by Pam Levine in 1982. Basically she agrees that there are "stages" of human development; however, those stages are experienced in cycles rather than in a linear way. She also identifies something I think is a key concept. When significant life events are experienced, we often experience cycles within cycles. In other words, we go back through and around the various stages further developing them.[4] Of course, this exciting concept offers

---

[4] Julie Hay, "Cycles of Development" *Family Issues*, 2003: 1–16. Journal online at:
http://www.ccedelaware.org/Libraries/HE_INFO/Cycles_of_Development.sflb.a

much more than can even begin to be discussed here. If you are interested, I encourage you to look up her work in the 1982 *Transactional Analysis Journal.* The point here is that the development of trust is significant in our early years as well as throughout our lives.

Adults, in fact professionals, have traditionally believed that "protecting" the child from certain information, such as not telling a six-year-old that her brother had died, is to the child's benefit. However, keeping this kind of significant information from the child only increases anxiety, decreases trust, and leads the child toward the path of withdrawal from others. Yes, this would have been difficult information for me to process no matter when or by whom I was told. However, the truth is, I knew someone died—I just didn't know if it was my father or my brother. When no one would tell me the truth, I felt like I had to decide who died. This burden was much more than I could carry, and I continually went back and forth between the two simply because I didn't want either to die. When I found out which one it was, I then felt guilty that I had ever chosen him. These are the issues that I finally was able to address constructively in pastoral counseling and spiritual direction throughout my thirties (which I will discuss further in this chapter).

My inability to trust became the foundational springboard for not sharing and not reaching out; instead, I sought isolation. The fact that I am an introvert surprises many people who know me well. Being introverted has been coupled with trust issues since childhood, which makes it a real challenge to push myself to trust and reach out. I'll never know if my being an introvert is natural or developed as a result of my experiences. Regardless, I gather my resources, my strength and energy, by taking quiet time for myself. During these times, which are now daily experiences, I play my instruments, cook, bake, meditate, read, mess with the dog's mind, or hang out in the water, my yard, and home. Being with others, especially groups of people, takes a tremendous amount of energy from me. At the same time, I thoroughly enjoy being with people. I also deeply want to open up to those I love, yet I continually discover that I'm not nearly as open as I think I am. However, discovering my trust issues and the fact that I'm an introvert has been significant in my process of

shx: Internet accessed 12 December 2010.

learning how to reach out.

My first appointment, that is, the first congregation that I served as pastor, had a staff of thirteen in addition to the senior pastor and myself, the associate pastor. In our desire to develop an environment of teamwork, we led the staff through the Steven Covey *7 Habits for Highly Effective People*. This proved to be an excellent experience for me. As I worked through the book, I realized that there were several habits that I practiced quite well and others with which I needed to gain more experience. One of these was his "Sphere of Influence."

In his Habit One, Covey talks about how proactive people take responsibility for their own lives. They use proactive language (I can, I will) rather than reactive language (I had to, I can't). Proactive people focus on the things that they can influence.

"Proactive people focus their efforts on their Circle of Influence. They work on the things they can do something about: health, children, problems at work. Reactive people focus their efforts in the Circle of Concern—things over which they have little or no control: the national debt, terrorism, the weather. Gaining an awareness of the areas in which we expend our energies in is a giant step in becoming proactive."[5]

One of my first learning curves was developing my "Sphere of Influence" by developing relationships with other people. Some people seem to be able to do this without thinking about it, but the truth is, good relationships are filled with intentionality, patience, and grace. I was in my forties before I realized that I'm a difficult person to get to know. The reason stems from my trust issues, being an introvert, and because I'm always listening to others' stories, encouraging others, helping others. Rarely do others ask to hear my story, and I don't think about offering it beyond a story here or there. People know me as a caring, compassionate, very assertive (some have other ways of saying this), and trustworthy person. They usually know that I have a strong personality, but they aren't real clear on what depth characterizes that personality.

During my tenure at my first church appointment, we conducted a major stewardship campaign to fund a million-dollar capital project.

---

[5] Steven Covey, *7 Habits of Highly Effective People* (Free Press, 2004), 83.

For this purpose we brought in a fund-raising company and consultants. After we had worked very closely with the consultants for about four months, as we were leaving a successful event, one of the consultants asked me something about myself. I responded by telling her of my background of growing up in the Pennsylvania Dutch community and highlighted a few of the significant lessons that I carried with me as a result. Both consultants suddenly came to a dead stop and were looking at me with wide eyes. The other consultant said to the first, "I told you, still waters run deep." While I took this as a compliment, I also realized that it was a sign that I needed to share more of myself with the people around me.

Over the years, I've learned improved ways of sharing my stories so people can get to know me; however, I'm still working on improving this part of my reaching out. I've also learned that people tend to make up what they don't know, especially when the unknown (me) holds a public or leadership office (clergy). People can be cruel, and there have been times where I preferred they just go away. But, God called me to ministry serving God's beloved (all people), so I had to find a way to relate. I must admit that I've found God's believers outside the institutional church much more receptive than those inside. Regardless, I've had to learn how to reach out and offer myself in both personal and professional relationships. I've also had to learn how to be gracious with myself as I make the inevitable mistakes through the learning process.

To do this, first I had to learn more about who I am and why I am who I am. Then I had to learn to love myself as I am, warts and all. My ugliest wart was anger, and I was deeply ashamed. As discussed earlier, when I was thirty, I started going to pastoral counseling to understand what this was all about and to figure out what to do about it. I went through almost ten years of counseling, self-reflection, and spiritual direction. Among the helpful resources, I found a book by David Augsburger immensely helpful: *Caring Enough to Confront*. All my life I have heard people condemn women as being a b____, bossy, aggressive, and abusive, when all they are doing is being assertive, expressing themselves with confidence and strength and providing appropriate leadership. What our society respects in males it often finds detestable in females. I felt like such a failure whenever a conflict arose. I thought that the lack of conflict was a sign of a person who could get along with people. Augsburger helped me understand this is not the case. In his preface he says, "It is not the conflicts that need to concern us, but how the conflicts are handled."[6] This was a huge revelation to me.

At the same time, I realized that I really was angry without knowing exactly how to resolve what I was angry about, which when combined with society's expectations shamed me. With the help of trusted and professional sources, I was able to find resolution over time. My shame slowly was broken down and away. I also studied anger and cultural expectations, developing a confidence in my skills, in my knowledge, and in myself. I grew in my ability to use anger in productive life-giving ways. I also grew in my ability to let the problems that others tried to impose on me remain their problems. While I celebrate my growth in these areas, I also recognize that I have even more potential, and I continue the work necessary.

All this has been important to my spiritual life, and my spiritual life has been important to this process. The only answer to the chicken/egg question is: yes. While exploring my ability to reach out, it was important to remember that I am a spiritual being and that reaching out is not just a two-dimensional process. Reaching out is multidimensional, involving self, others, the Divine, and creation. The ability to withstand a significant amount of vulnerability is essential to this process also.

I believe that vulnerability has been a part of my issue with being more open about myself with others. Rejection is not something I deal with well. I've also experienced a tremendous amount of loss in my life. My husband of five months divorced me following the train wreck. I can't tell you the devastation I felt on top of all the other losses due to the train wreck. In addition to this, I was in the train because we were going to my father's funeral. During this incredibly painful time, I had put some of my feelings into words:

---

[6] David Augsburger, *Caring Enough to Confront: How to understand and express your deepest feelings toward others* (Ventura, CA: Regal Books, 1973), 6.

The Hole

Life stinks
Pain
I don't really mean it
but it hurts
How could I be such an idiot
I believed him
He proposed
He took vows to love me through ups and downs
5 months later a horrible thing happened
and suddenly … . The only reason he married me
was because he was lonely?
When did he lie
When he took vows
Or when he broke my heart
Some think I shouldn't be so upset
That I'm obsessed

I think they're crazy
My god! I'm in shock
How stark can it be
I thought I was married
I thought I was loved
I came back to life
And
It
Was
Gone
Our dreams
Our hopes
Our us
Our future
All gone

My love stands alone, with emptiness
Unfulfilled
Anger has set in the void

But where to go?
He doesn't care, it makes no difference
My heart can't buy it
How is it that he never loved
He says he married me out of loneliness
Why, why did he say
I love you
I take these vows
I want you in my life
You are my soul mate

Why … if it was only loneliness?
Why did he say
I want a divorce it's not about you
I just can't live with anyone
And I don't want to be married

Why … if he loved me
Why
Why did he push me out
Shut me out
and bring another in?

I struggled with the paradox of this extreme distrust and anger that seemed to pervade my soul. I felt totally abandoned and betrayed by everyone. The only thing that held me together was that I knew the one who loved me into being was on my side and would never abandon me. The Divine was the only thing or one I could trust and hold on to. (Well, the Divine and my dog.) Anything tangible was to be protected against. I didn't even trust myself—especially my body.

We've all been burned. At least, I don't know of a single human being who has never been deeply hurt by a relationship. Getting to the place where we can feel even an interest in relating with another person takes a tremendous amount of work. Of course, we need some time to withdraw, lick our wounds, and sleep in the fetal position. But we don't want to spend too much time hiding or it could become our own personal prison of death. One of my favorite "Rose Is Rose" cartoons was when she was despondent over a betrayal. The artist drew Rose in a deep, dark hole surrounded with a circular cement block wall that extended high above her head. There was a tiny square opening covered with prison bars at the top. Rose was crumbled on the bottom with her head hanging.

Have you ever been there? I sure have had my share of pity parties. There comes a point where we are no longer the victim of another; rather we become our own victim. Some people choose to stay there, because to climb out of that deep dark hole can be terrifying. Not everyone has the support system (internally or externally) needed to make the climb. Knowing and trusting our strengths is crucial to this process. Hopefully there is someone nearby who is willing to reach out to us with the healing grace we need.

Even though I had not been able to enter into a meaningful relationship with a man for many years afterward, I hadn't given up; healing progressed. I felt ready for a real relationship and very much wanted one. However, I didn't know just how vulnerable I could allow myself to be. The fact that I understood what had led me to this emotional place was very important. It was even more important that I had accepted that this was okay. I worked on building my ability to trust and improving my ability to protect myself.

Often, since then, I've reflected on my relationship with God, realizing how often I mess up. God has sustained a tremendous amount of hurt by choosing to continue to love me through it all. I'm fascinated by this. Where does God's reservoir come from? While it's blatantly clear to me that I can't even begin to match God's fidelity; I can learn from my experience of this kind of love.

I've learned much about codependency. All loving relationships are codependent to a point. However, there comes a point when it becomes unhealthy. That point is when we lose ourselves in another person. In my dissertation discussion of my theological process, which I call *DNA of Life*, I talk about intimacy as a key component to my theological process. My description begins:

"I don't know how to define it other than illusive, comforting, desirable relating with not only others but also self and creation. I think of Job's friends

sitting with him in the midst of ashes for days, crying with him, not asking or talking or correcting, but sitting with and crying with … fully being with. This is intimacy. It is a quiet caring for another that warms the heart of both. It is community. A deep appreciation for self even with your flaws, a kind understanding wrapped in love, a desire to know and be known that opens the heart of both."[7]

How are you with intimacy? Do you tend to cross the line into unhealthy codependence or maybe the line into being nonrelational? Wellness depends on balance. Perhaps the Tao concept of Yin-Yang is helpful. Huston Smith describes the Yin-Yang as such:

"This polarity sums up all of life's basic oppositions: good/evil, active/passive, positive/negative, light/dark, summer/winter, male/female. But though the halves are in tension, they are not flatly opposed; they complement and balance each other. Each invades the other's hemisphere and takes up its abode in the deepest recess of its partner's domain. And in the end both find themselves resolved by the circle that surrounds them, the Tao in its eternal wholeness. In the context of that wholeness, the opposites appear as no more than phases in an endless cycling process, for each turns incessantly into its opposite, exchanging places with it. Life does not move onward and upward toward a fixed pinnacle or pole. It bends back upon itself to come, full circle, to the realization that all is one and all is well."[8]

The book *The Joy Luck Club* beautifully illustrates the concept of Yin-Yang or balance as it explores the male/female relationship, mother/daughter relationship, and Chinese/American cultural relationships among many other examples of the women's struggles to achieve balance in their lives.[9] Day and night also beautifully demonstrate Yin-Yang. Dawn and dusk show how they are parts of one another and continually cycle in the midst of and regardless of all else. Intimacy invites a deep honoring of another within while the other does the same. In balance this is an experience of life-giving

[7] The Rev. Pamela Feeser, D.Min. *Buying the Vineyard: Different Options for Living, Playing, and Hoping in Non-violence and Safety: DOLPHINS.* Miami, FL: (Dissertation for doctoral work at South Florida Center for Theological Studies, 2003), 47.

[8] Huston Smith, *The World's Religion* (San Francisco: Harper, 1991), 214.

[9] Tan, Amy. *The Joy Luck Club* (New York: Penguin), 2006.

love, co-creation of living anew. Reaching out to others with honesty and grace, opening our hearts and minds all while retaining our own identity and celebrating growth and new life born of this relationship honors the one who reaches out to us minute by minute, day after day with endless life-giving graceful love.

Reaching out, however, is about much more than just reaching out to other people. We are also in relationship with the world around us. As I write this, my community and my country struggle through the horror and fury of watching the earth bleed oil in the Gulf waters following irresponsible, despicable human behavior. We have no idea how to fix this, and we clearly are not moving fast enough. The Deepwater Horizon oil spill began with an explosion on April 20, 2010, the largest oil spill ever in the United States. Not only are people's lives destroyed, but the earth, the poor earth cries out in pain. Fish die, toxins poison the water, plant life suffocates, birds drown in oil-drenched feathers.

Our arrogance has brought us here. How dare we choose to dig holes five thousand feet underwater without being absolutely certain that explosions and oil spills could not possibly happen. Perhaps you're thinking, well now there's a Pollyanna view of oil drilling. However, my point is how dare we think that it's okay to do such a thing. Maybe it's complacency, arrogance, selfishness, greed; whatever it is it's not acceptable.

When the Creator of this beautiful earth commissioned us to "fill the earth with people and bring it under your control. Rule over the fish in the ocean, the birds in the sky, and every animal on the earth," (Genesis 1:28–), the Source of All Being did not mean that we are to rule with arrogance. God is not into power and control issues; God abhors abuse of any form. God was commanding us to be in relationship with the earth, fish, birds, and creation in such a way that the gift of life would be honored and sustained. This doesn't mean that we aren't to eat or drink or use transportation or invent things. It means that as we use the elements of creation to sustain life, we must do it in a way that honors the very thing we are using and honors the Creator too. Stewardship is much more than an action; it must be an expression of one's relationship with creation.

Native Americans have beautiful traditions in this regard. A Native American proverb goes: "Treat the earth well: it was not given to you by your parents; it was loaned to you by your children. We do not inherit the Earth from our ancestors; we borrow it from our children." While some Christian theologians, such as Tillich, believe that creation is flawed just as humanity is; Native Americans believe that creation is pure and good. The United Methodist Book of Worship shares a beautiful Opening Prayer by the Dakota Tribe:

Grandfather, Great Spirit, you have always been and before you nothing has been. There is no one to pray to but you. The star nations all over the heaven are yours, and yours are the grasses of the earth. You are older than all need, older than all pain and prayer. Grandfather, Great Spirit, fill us with light. Give us strength to understand and eyes to see. Teach us to walk the soft earth as relatives to all that live. Help us, for without you we are nothing. Amen.[10]

Just as with any group of early people, the Native Americans observed the world around them and sought to explain the mysteries they witnessed. Their explanations are represented in their beautiful rituals and mythology where they refer to Father Sun, Mother Corn, and Brother Bear. These references indicate the strong familial relationship they felt and nurtured with the rest of creation. They understood themselves as equals with creation; sharing responsibilities to and with one another. These stories are not literal; rather they represent relationship, lessons, explanations that are passed on from generation to generation through story and ritual. Along with this style of expression comes a basic philosophy of self-identity that guides future actions and decision making.[11]

St. Francis of Assisi is known as the patron saint of animals and the environment. He lived in twelfth-century Italy. His "Canticle of the Sun" is revered by many even today:

O most high, omnipotent, good Lord God, to you belong praise, glory, honor

---

[10] E. Russell Carter, *The Gift is Rich* (New York, NY; The Friendship Press, 1955), 59.

[11] Hartley Burr Alexander, *Native American Mythology* (Mineola, NY: Dover Publications, Inc., 2005), xi-xx.

and all blessing. For our brother the sun, who is our day and who brings us the light, who is fair and radiant with a very great splendor; Praise be our Lord. For our sister the moon, and for the stars, which you have set clear and lovely in heaven; for our brother the wind, and for air and clouds, calms and all weather; for our sister water, who serves us and is humble and precious and chaste; for our brother fire, by whom you light up the night, and who is fair and merry, and very mighty and strong; for our mother the earth, who sustains us and keeps us, and brings forth various fruits, and flowers of many colors, and grass; for all those who pardon one another for your love's sake, and who bear weakness and tribulation; blessed are they who peaceably shall endure, walking by your most holy will; for you, O Most High, shall give them a crown. Praise and bless the Lord, and give thanks unto God, and serve God with great humility. Amen.[12]

Now we can read the words of St. Francis as well as the Native American liturgy as simply poetic. It would make us feel good and happy. Maybe we would think it's a pretty poem. However, we might as well pour oil in the lake as we recite such poetry. We cannot skim across the surface of life and reach out at the same time. If this poetry is an extension of, an expression of, a manifestation of who we are in relationship to creation; if this poetry claims the voice of our soul and leads our being into action; if this poetry worships God then we can do nothing less than honor the holiness of all creation. So why don't we?

Romanticizing life is an easy out for us. The lay leader of one of the congregations I've served was speaking. He shared a true story that had happened in his kitchen that week. He and his wife were in the middle of remodeling. As she prepared supper one night, a squirrel scurried across the floor and she screamed. Her husband came running as she climbed the kitchen chair. He chased the squirrel, which ran behind the stove, jumped up on a cord, and stuck his head in a hole in the wall. Suddenly, with his feet on the cord and his head in the hole the squirrel calmed completely down. Noticing the sudden radical change in the squirrel's demeanor, the lay leader and his wife stopped. There stood the squirrel confident as ever with his head in the hole. As long as he didn't see them, he must have figured they didn't see him and he was safe. Now that's romanticizing

---

[12] Public Domain; source: *The United Methodist Book of Worship* © 1992; The United Methocist Publishing House.

life.

Of course we're going to fall short; however, that's no excuse for not even trying. Reaching out requires vulnerability on our part, which can become painful but at the same time brings incredible joy and growth to life. Romanticizing life is what blinds us from the warning signs that the Deepwater Horizon catastrophes are about to take place. When we properly attend to our relationship with creation, we cannot allow ourselves to turn a blind eye or deaf ear to these signs. In fact, we will seek them out and lower our defenses in the interest of the greater good when our focus on that which is greater than ourselves yet includes ourselves. We can clearly detect where we are placing the weight of our decisions by what bothers us the most.

Activity 3

Where do you need to reach out in your life?
Relationship development
Receiving and giving
Asking to receive and to give
Development of grace and forgiveness
Communication expansion

CHAPTER FIVE : INTENTIONAL LIVING

Even the word music is the most beautiful word to me. The sound of the word, even the look of the word just sings beauty. Ever since I was two years old, music has been where my soul has resided. In fact, through music, my soul most clearly and fully expresses life as I experience it.

When I was a toddler, I remember going around the yard experimenting with my voice. I would try to see how high and how low I could go, how loudly and how quietly. Apparently I drove my mom up the wall. One day she told me to stop screaming. Looking back, I certainly can't blame her, but at the time I was offended. I just didn't realize how horribly irritating such high screeches could be. I was amazed at what the voice could do and how I could make it do things just by thinking about it. Today, I'm not such a good vocalist, but I'm an accomplished instrumentalist.

My Pennsylvania Dutch community taught me that God gives each of us gifts, and the best way to appreciate God is to perfect those gifts and use them for God's glory throughout our lives. Clearly God had gifted me with this amazing blessing called music. I started out at two years old dancing, and then at eight I began to play music through a variety of musical instruments, my favorite being the flute. I have to chuckle even today when I say that I'm going to play my music. I mean something very different than my friends. They turn on the radio; I turn on my heart.

In high school there was never a question—I was going into music. During the various hospital stays I had following the Labor Day accident years earlier, I had come across a lady who would come to the hospital regularly. She had a room filled with instruments to make music with, and she would invite me in as part of my healing process. I deeply loved this and looked forward to it. I had decided that I wanted to use my gift of music in the same way. I wanted to help people to heal physically, emotionally, educationally by inviting them into the world of music. However, the only profession in music that I was aware of was teaching.

This has turned out to be a best-case scenario for me because apparently God also has blessed me with the love of and ability to teach. I had several excellent colleges of music to choose from. I was even approached by one with a full music scholarship. Unfortunately, the scholarship wasn't from the college I chose. My college, West Chester State College (WCSC), was excellent for music, and had a top-notch flute teacher. It was just far enough away from home as well as just close enough. I had attended marching band camp at the college to learn how to be the drum major for my high school marching band and had fallen in love with the campus. The oak trees formed this beautiful canvas over the streets while adorable squirrels bounced from tree to tree. Swope Music Hall was a dream. There were eighty-eight practice rooms and numerous classrooms. I would walk down the hallways to the creative chaos of musicians galore. How fulfilling that was for me.

I wanted to honor God, I wanted to go to WCSC, and I was going to do whatever it took to follow through. First I had to take my SATs. My score was high enough. I also needed to learn how to play piano and sight sing. My high school band director and choral director helped me out with these things. Next I had to audition. I was given a date in October 1977. It just so happened that the night before my audition, our marching band was competing and we didn't get back until around midnight. The college was two hours away, and I was going to have to drive myself there by eight in the morning.

Well, I got there. I played Mozart's Concerto in G for flute, sang an aria from the Messiah, played something very basic on piano, took my seashore test (a hearing test for musicians), and was tested on various other musical skills. I drove home down Route 30 into Hanover, my hometown. I had no idea how I did, but I felt good. I knew I did the best I could. I waited, impatient to hear back from the college.

One day following our after-school marching practice, my band director asked me to stay so he could talk with me. It turned out the letter had come. My mother had opened it and brought it in to my band director so he could talk with me. Prior to talking with me, he had made a few phone calls to WCSC for clarification. I was accepted into the school academically. However, because I was self-taught as a musician, they were not sure that I had the ability to discipline myself to be taught by a professional. My skills were definitely good enough, but they wanted me to get a private teacher to study with for several months and then audition again. All I heard was, you're not good enough, we reject you, go away.

I was devastated. If that wasn't enough, my father had come to pick me up after practice, and because I wasn't there waiting for him (I was talking to the director), he left. I wanted to die. I hid down one of the hallways in an alcove and cried my heart out. I just wanted to disappear. How could I be such a failure? Here God gave me this gift and look at what I was doing with it—nothing. I curled up in a ball and tried to hide from God and everyone else. After I thought everyone had gone, I slipped out the back door. I didn't know where I was going, but I wanted to go away where no one would know me and I could disappear. The next thing I knew, my band director pulled up alongside me in his car and asked me where I was going and why was I walking. I lied and told him I was walking home. He said, "No, you're not. Get in." He took me back to the school, called my mom, and had her come get me. I didn't speak to a single person for at least a month.

Somehow I found out about a private flute teacher in a town forty-five minutes away. I scheduled lessons, and what a joy that turned out to be. He taught me how to breathe and use different tonguing techniques, and he was able to play duets not only at my level but beyond. I had never come across someone like that. Learning from him was so invigorating. I looked forward to lessons, worked hard, and auditioned again.

This time, I was accepted on probation as a music student. I was insulted because I just knew I was good enough to be a full student. The first week of classes I challenged my probation by auditioning again and was accepted as a full music student. It turned out that I was ranked tenth out of the sixty flute majors in the college and got to play in the flute ensemble. Now I was ready to learn and develop my wonderful divine gift more completely. Music continues to be the joy of my living, my fullest expression of who I am, and one of my most effective expressions of ministry.

Think back to a time when you had your mind set on what you wanted and you didn't get it. What did you do? What do you do? How do you decide what is important to you? How far will you go to accomplish your desires?

Living our lives is the most important thing we will ever do. Deciding how to live our lives is the most important thing we will ever decide. What are the things that you allow to influence your decision making? Have you intentionally thought about this?

In my example, the things that influenced my decision were my experience and love of music and my relationship with God as shaped by the teachings of my community of faith. I had other things that I was good at, in fact I excelled at: languages, math, and cooking/baking. But my heart was with music, and I was convinced that this was a God-given gift. I could have been successful in any of the fields, but my passion was for music.

People often say that they know that something is the God-given path because everything just falls into place. I cannot say that. My mother did everything she could to clear the path for my music during my childhood. She had to run interference for me with my father and even with some of the people at my church. Then my decision to go to college met with all kinds of obstacles. My parents had no money to help me with my education. I had to find scholarships, grants, jobs, and loans to pay my way through. I was the first person in my family to even go to college. Getting accepted into the music program was only the beginning of my struggles. After graduating with a teaching degree and a Pennsylvania teaching license as a band director, I discovered that school districts in the Pennsylvania Dutch community were not too keen on female band directors. So a very good question is: what is it that made me believe so fully that this was what God wanted me to do?

The "tried and true" belief that if God wills it the whole thing will come easily just didn't prove true for me. Once again the question becomes, how did I know this was a direction that God was leading me in and not just what I wanted? Ultimately, when I'm trying to discern the appropriate action, decision, or behavior, the question that I try to always ask is: What is the best life-giving decision for all involved? I focus on life-giving because if I had to choose one characteristic of the divine that is all encompassing, it would be "life-giving." God, Creator, Source of All Being, Redeemer, Wisdom: these are all names we use that point toward life-giving characteristics. Divine guidance always leads us to true living, full living, life-giving experiences. As we continue to grow in our relationship with the One Who loved Us into Being, we develop the gracious gift of spreading that life-giving love to those with whom we relate. We also begin to accept the responsibility to share that life-giving love with the relational creation around us.

I also believe that my decisions, actions, and behaviors must always include others, because just as our Creator is relational, so are we. Even though, I literally live on an island, I can't possibly live like I'm an island to myself. Life cannot possibly be lived in a vacuum. Not only do we need one another, we need creation itself and vice versa. Even our understanding of God as the Triune God expresses our belief that within God's self there is significant relationship.

One of the most beautiful and creative ways of talking about this is found in a treasure of a book, The Shack, by William Paul Young. I especially love his description of the Trinity in the kitchen preparing a meal. He celebrates their differences and their honoring of one another's uniqueness. At one point his character, Mack, asks the question, "You don't have to eat do you?" And the response is "We don't have to do anything," which Mack follows up with, "Then why do you?" The response is, "To be with you, honey. You need to eat, so what better excuse to be together." He goes on to describe the joyful and respectful banter within the Trinity. This is one of the most beautiful, deep, and creative books written in our lifetime. I encourage everyone to treat themselves to his insightful book.

Music has always given me life and healing, helping me to develop ways to share that same beauty with others. The difficulties that have challenged my journey through the years have only served to help me grow and strengthen. Of course, this is because I choose to use them that way rather than to allow them to victimize me. Throughout it all, I've always felt God's supporting presence. That certainly doesn't mean that there weren't times when I felt sorry for myself and fully expected others to do the same.

I remember a time during my junior year in college when my flute teacher wrote a nasty letter just tearing me to pieces. I was devastated to the point that I went to the Music Department office to withdraw from school. My friends ran to one of the professors that was well loved and respected and told her what was happening. She was waiting for me. I still remember her high-pitched voice calling my name from down the hallway and the familiar clickity click of her high heels on the floor as she ran toward me. There was no way I would ever disrespect her, so I stopped and went to her. She grabbed my hand and quickly led me to a practice room. She encouraged me to explain what had happened, and then she read the letter.

It turned out that my flute teacher was a close personal friend of hers. She expressed disappointment in her friend and promised to run interference for me. She sat, ignoring her class, listening to me, comforting me and helping me determine a plan of action that included finishing my degree and staying in the School of Music. In the following weeks, she stayed true to her word and worked out the difficulties on my behalf. She secured a new flute teacher for me and gained a special place in my heart for life. This experience was terribly painful and embarrassing for me; however, the positive lessons I gained because I didn't give up have stayed with me informing my life-giving decisions ever since.

Music has always been the clearest, most complete communication between me and the one who gave me life. It has never been about how others have reacted or responded. It's always been about what gives me life, so I can give it back. Music has carved the pathway for my ministry over the years. Oddly enough, that pathway has led to my current work in community health ministries rather than a full-time vocation in music.

Of course I've made, and continue to make, wrong choices. However, I also continue to listen to divine direction as best I can. I can't always tell the difference between what I want and what God is calling me to do. But I've learned that if I keep attentive to my relationship with my Creator, eventually things seem to move in the right direction. My soul seems to know when this happens. There's a quiet confidence and strength that empowers my living when this happens. My contribution is simply to be attentive and willing. It's amazing how divine blessings flow when the path is open.

There's a difference between intentional living and determined living. With intentional living, the whole of one's situation is weighed along with the numerous options and specific choices are made based on the depths of who that individual understands herself to be. With determined living, the focus is narrowly and fearfully defined leading to reaction-based actions. Determined living doesn't always lead to life, if at all. Whereas intentional living definitely includes determination and passion, in this case there is balance and clear decision making that continually takes place. This cycling of balanced decision making, focus on a chosen goal, and continual reevaluation of the process creates a life-giving movement into greater depth of being.

After the train wreck, I was terrified. In fact, I was absolutely convinced that I was going to die for several years. I was determined to stay alive. As a result, I reacted, usually violently, to absolutely everything. For at least the first year, I was petrified that if I fell asleep I would die. In fact, that did happen several times during the first few days in the hospital.

I remember two near-death experiences that I had during that horrid time. I had been bleeding internally for two days. The doctors discovered this when I collapsed due to multiple pulmonary embolisms hitting both of my lungs. They put me on Coumadin to break up the clots. When I wasn't getting better but instead continued to get worse, they finally figured out that I was bleeding into my abdomen due to internal cuts from the four breaks in my lumbar spine. I ended up receiving ten units of blood before I was out of danger. I died as they tried to insert a filter in my vena cava to stop the process of clots. For two weeks, I was in critical condition in ICU with tubes coming out of every possible part of my body. I can't express how raw and vulnerable I felt.

While my memories during this time are only a few seconds here or there, I've been told some of the things I did. Apparently, one day I saw a housekeeper cleaning the floors of the ICU and was utterly convinced he was there to kill me. I demanded that he be removed. I was determined to live and was reacting to everything around me. I wasn't capable of making balanced decisions. Desperation and fear permeated my every breath.

Later, when I was moved to a step-down room, those poor people who lovingly come into your room to take samples of blood so the doctors can make balanced life-promoting decisions unfortunately were the recipients of my determination. My body was completely purple, a shade of purple I never care to see again. The pain, even with morphine, was excruciating. The fear, vulnerability, and terror swirled around me gnashing their vicious canines. As the lab person gently walked up to the side of my bed, I was terrified they were going to take all the blood I had left and their needles hurt. I reacted. Through clenched teeth and blaring eyes I screamed with all I had,

"If you stick me with that one more time, I'm going to punch you." The next time I woke up, I had a central line going directly into my heart. I can't tell you how terrified I was then.

Basically, for several years I was so terrified and determined to stay alive I couldn't think straight. Of course, this was all symptomatic of PTSD, which unfortunately became chronic. My body was so horrendously beat up and damaged that many injuries took months, even years to diagnose. The reason was that some less severe injuries, like massive nerve damage, were covered up by more severe and life-threatening injuries. When the more severe injuries began to calm down, the under layers of injury were revealed over the course of the following three years.

Each time, I reexperienced the trauma of the train wreck all over again. Then on top of this were the emotional and inter-relational injuries. It would be years before I could even begin to get to a place where I could think about the possibility of mature, balanced decision making. I owe a great debt to my numerous doctors during this time. My lawyer tells me I had twenty-three of them. Some of the number was due to the numerous types of doctors I needed. A good portion was due to the fact that I was bouncing off the walls (figuratively this time) and just impossible to be around for any length of time. I was slowly killing the very life that I was so determined to save.

Fortunately, I had a strong relationship with God prior to the train wreck, which kept me focused throughout. In fact, during the first year after the train wreck, I was finishing up on my dissertation for my doctor of ministry degree. I was not able to read or put together a complete sentence for months and months. How I finished my dissertation and received my degree in June of 2003, I have no clue. However, my topic was "ministry in domestic violence," and the primary Scripture I used was Jeremiah 32. Jeremiah has a wonderful understanding of God as the fountain of living water that has so completely flowed through my life in the years since. It's not even just a river of living water as John talks about, but an actual fountain. I picture a magnificent shower of water shooting up from the center, cascading down with its refreshing life-giving breath on everything willing to receive it. Dancing around the fountain, I see life flourishing and growing in a brilliant array of greens. A fragrance of joy and hope permeates the air as new life buds forth. This is the vision my Creator gave me as I struggled to reach out for just a drop, knowing that God's right hand was holding me through it all.

Because I knew the importance of making measured decisions and helping myself heal in ways that were true to who I am as God's beloved, I kept bringing myself back to this vision as well as others to guide me through. As I said earlier, I am no saint; there were plenty of times when I made wrong decisions and hurt myself as well as others. By accepting and sharing the grace of agape with myself, I was able to move forward centimeter by centimeter.

As I stumbled through this process, I was blessed from time to time with people who may or may not have realized the blessings they brought to me and my process of coming back to life. My one orthopedic surgeon (I had three of them) provided healing in ways expected but also by the way he was so unbelievably patient with me, the way he listened, the way he chose to save my leg despite all the odds, the way he simply was with me. I wasn't just a crushed leg to him; I was a fellow beloved child of God who was experiencing hell on earth.

My supervisor at work also shared this view of me. He saved my job and held it for me for years until I was able to come back. He could have fired me numerous times simply because of my PTSD behavior, but grace prevailed. He made sure my insurance paperwork was all completed without my knowing a thing. He got people in the system to donate paid time off to make sure I kept getting paychecks. My lawyer tolerated my frantic terrified phone calls with grace. He intercepted all my creditors so I wouldn't lose my PTSD-filled mind and emotions as well as self-respect. A neighbor contacted me when she discovered that I had no transportation to my numerous (at least fifteen per week) doctor's appointments and proceeded to take me to every single one. For over a year she did this with a smile and would accept nothing in return. The blessings that others provided in the midst of my hell were true miracles and way too numerous to list. I'm quite sure there are many more that I don't even recall, in the same way that I've forgotten much more than I can possibly recall.

Intentional living means making it a point to recognize and hold in tension these dichotomies of pain and grace as you strive to discern the healthy path for your living. It certainly isn't clean or neat or easy or clear. It just is. The meaning of it all will only come to you as you continue to heal and reflect and grow. There is no formula, no program, no pattern that fits all; there is only you and life and God and now.

One of the most important lessons for me was to build my ability to share the grace and forgiveness with myself that I so readily give to others. Until I began to share this with myself, I was not able to heal at all or to live with intentionality. My psychologist was a huge help in this area. She and I had worked together for several years prior to the train wreck. Interestingly enough, while we respected one another's skills and professionalism, we did not like one another. I went to her in spite of this because I knew she could handle the seriousness of my situation and my psyche. Today we love one another and have even greater respect for one another. She is a Christian and is not afraid to hold me accountable to the Christian ideals I hold. She certainly is not afraid of my anger and rage—the ugly side of my healing. And she has never let me get away with only going partway in sharing the gracious love that I have for others with myself.

Four people died in the train wreck; I was told that those four people had been in my sleeper car when they died. I could not forgive myself for not being able to give comfort to these people while they struggled through those moments. Of course, most people would question why I would think I should have been there for them. I'm a pastor, a spiritual leader, one who has sat with many people and families through the dying process. It's something that is simply a part of my divine calling. I've always been able to provide pastoral support for others regardless of what I might be going through personally. I've always been able to set aside my own concerns when my pastoral support has been needed and deal with my stuff later. However, this wasn't the only reason I couldn't forgive myself. I was also suffering from survivor's guilt.

As a result of my inability to forgive myself and offer myself the grace I needed to move forward in a healthy way, I had become extremely angry and hateful toward myself. I had become determined to push this aside and just get over it. To help me move from determined living to intentional living, my psychologist helped me struggle with the realization that I needed to not only forgive myself but also to provide the pastoral support that was so important to me. By writing a letter to the people who died in the sleeper car, I was able to access healing as well as gracious forgiveness:

A Letter to the people who died in the sleeper car:

I am so very sad and sickened by what happened to you. I was in your car and left just before it happened. I'm glad I left, because I'm happy to be alive. At the same time, I feel guilty because I was the lucky one and I'm happy I was lucky. I am not happy about what happened to you though. I really want you to know that. Please understand these are raw feelings; they are not thought through or logical in any way. I wonder if the maintenance man/men who were supposed to take care of the upkeep of that track feel any remorse. Their carelessness caused your death. I don't get the sense that anyone at Amtrak has any remorse. They have refused to accept any responsibility so far. We all have to take them to court to make them accept any responsibility. But I know there are a few passengers who definitely feel terrible about what happened to you. I hope your families carry on your memories in helpful ways. I hope they are able to honor your memory. I know it must be terrible for them.

The thing that haunts me the most is the hell you must have experienced just before dying. I know what mine was like. I'm sorry you didn't have a chance to fight back. The shock, horror, sickening cries of twisting metal, the realization of powerlessness against the odds, the fear, the lack of time … you didn't have a chance … you weren't given a chance. Being thrown so violently like you were nothing … but you were something, you were something vitally important … you were you. Please know that you were important. Please know that whatever you did in life is accepted as the very best you were able to do. If you are regretful for things that you did or didn't do … there is space for you and grace to heal. You didn't die alone. You are not forgotten. Whatever the answers are to the questions of the afterlife, you know them now. Those answers are full of grace and acceptance and fulfillment of life. I'm sorry you didn't get to continue to live out your goals/passions/whatever it was that was important to you. That would be very hard for me to accept. In fact, when I die I will probably need you to remind me of some of this too. I know the excruciating pain—rather torture—of healing after this train wreck in life. I hope and pray that healing is much easier and more complete in the afterlife.

My mind is jumping around writing this and I know that I'm blocking my feelings because it just hurts too much to be in touch with them right now. I allow myself glimpses and the pain in my chest is instantaneous and the tears blur my eyes. I am so sorry for what happened to you. You deserved better. This was an injustice and you were victims. You are probably dealing with this better than I am. It's always easier when it's you and not someone else. What I really want is for you to know that someone who doesn't even know you cares deeply about what happened to you. I want to take away the injustice and pain that you suffered, but I know that I can't. My faith tells me that while God doesn't take away bad things that happen to us, he does heal the wounds and helps us to find life-affirming answers to these scars in our living. I don't know how, but I believe that life continues after death but in a way that is closer to our Creator. I'm sorry to impose my beliefs on you, but actually this is my hell that we are talking about anyway. I do believe yours is over. My frustration is that I couldn't be there to support you while you were going through yours. I could not have prevented it, but if I were able to be there I could have supported you and would have. Please know that.

Writing this, I'm realizing that a large portion of my tears and, yes, emotional pain is due to the fact that I realize two things more than ever: 1. that I've been given, yet one more time, the awesome gift of life; and 2. I now understand better than ever before, once again, how astounding the gift of life is. This is a true treasure, as I knew before but know even more completely now. And it is a treasure that we can give to one another in countless ways every moment of our living… or we can take it away.

Thank you for the life that you gave during yours. I will continue to develop my abilities to give life to others and myself during mine.

—Pam

Once again I discovered that confession is good for the soul, and that forgiveness and grace make the world a whole better place to live. This release helped me to move that much closer to living intentionally. It also equipped me with yet one more experience of success in facing my demons and gaining the ability and confidence to once again make healthy choices for my own life and living.

ACTIVITY 4

1. What roadblocks are standing in your way of intentional living? Are you able to recognize when you are reacting and when you are responding? If you're a human being, you can be assured that you will both react and respond depending on what else is going on in your life at the time. However, it's important for you to claim the truth of what you do most often. A trusted, objective third party would be helpful here. Someone who does not have emotional attachments to you and is mature with your best interests in mind is the best person to ask for help in this reflection.

2. Once you are able to determine if reacting or responding is your current "norm," you can move on to the next step, recognizing what is going on inside you when you become reactionary. What are your internal/external physical symptoms? What are you feeling? As you become more aware of these "red flags" you will learn what you need to do to alleviate these behaviors so that you will be able to make appropriate and healthy choices/decisions. As you gain these skills, you will become better equipped to live with intentionality.

☐

CHAPTER SIX : RELATIONAL EXPANSION OF WORLDVIEW

Where I grew up, I had the privilege of being part of the Pennsylvania Dutch community. My family is Pennsylvania Dutch; we're part of the Church People. My home was surrounded by farms, and for a long time was a farmhouse. Hay, corn, apple orchards, sour cherry trees, cows, chickens, and pigs were among my everyday experience. I love the breathtaking smell of the apple orchards. I love going to the farmers' market. In fact, every time I go back home now, I go to the various farmers' markets and buy fresh produce and traditional candies to enjoy during my stay. My neighbors' who were Amish; other Church People; and Mennonites (all of the Pennsylvania Dutch tradition) would bring fresh-baked pies, breads, cookies, and cakes along with freshly picked produce.

At home, Mom always had fresh sour cherry, apple, or strawberry-rhubarb pies in the oven. With three younger brothers, my father, and me, the pies never lasted long once they came out of the oven. We got fresh eggs right from under the chicken, and our milk was so fresh we had to shake it before pouring to mix the cream back into the milk. I gobbled up the skills of baking, cooking, quilting, sewing, and crocheting. I especially love cooking and baking today much to the pleasure of my friends and coworkers.

My high school had four tracts we could take: academic, business, general, and agriculture. In fact, my high school owned a working farm right next to the school that the agriculture students farmed. To this day, I am able to tell what animals a farm has simply by the smell.

Now isn't that an exciting skill!

When I was three years old, my four-year-old brother and I seized the day. Mom had briefly gone inside our three-story farmhouse and we were outside in the yard. The rule was that we were not to go past the creek in the middle of the yard. But we both just loved cows, and the cows were in the barn. The barn was on the other side and … well, we ran. The pen around the cows was a cement wall; however, the gate was wooden two-by-fours. Duffy climbed the fence, and I followed my big brother's steps—into the pen with the cows we went. Wow! Now these were big cows. I was so fascinated. I believe the cows were too. They turned around and looked at us looking at them. They were so calm and gentle. I was so enchanted I didn't even notice the smell. I don't even remember breathing.

Suddenly Mom was at the gate. Thinking back, I can't even imagine how terrified she must have been, not to mention stunned at how we got inside to begin with. With amazing calm, she asked us how we got in. Duffy explained that we had climbed the gate. Mom looked at her three-year-old daughter and back at her four-year-old son as she tried to process that. We must have been a sight. Mom was terrified that any sudden movements or sounds would bring the cows forward and we would be trampled. Duffy and I were joyfully clueless. I don't remember how we got out of the pen, but I do know that we were safe and the cows, unlike us, behaved.

I have always been in touch with domestic and farm animals, the land, crops, the weather, woods, hills, nature, and the importance of my relationship with it all. My faith community and surrounding culture taught me stewardship not just of my own but also of my neighbors. We cared about, participated in, and prayed for the care of the farms, the dams, and one another's health. I was very fortunate in what my community taught me.

However, there were things I didn't know about. I remember the first time I found out that people came in different colors. It was in the mid-sixties, and I was seven years old. Mom, Dad, and I went to church that morning. I was holding Mom's hand and as we walked in the back door, I saw that the back pew was filled with people and their skin was black! I had never seen black skin before and had just spent the last year recovering from the terrible accident that took my brother, so I knew pain, both physical and emotional. I recognized the pain in the faces of these people. I was convinced they had been burned in a fire and that was the source of the pain they were in. I felt so sorry for them. I wanted to go to them and tell them that God loved them and it would get better. I wanted them to know that I felt for their pain.

My poor parents had no idea what my problem was. Mom had to practically drag me down the aisle. I insisted on walking backward so I could stare at the "burned people" in the back pew. When we arrived at our pew, I scooted in between Mom and Dad, kneeling but still looking back at the poor burned people in the back pew. I was convinced that if I thought hard enough they would hear my words of compassion and prayer for them. Mom tried to get me to straighten out. She told me that staring was rude and plopped me around. Immediately I wanted to turn again. I was convinced they were in pain and wanted them to know that God and I cared.

If only I had known the true source of their pain. I can only imagine what everyone else thought was going on. It was many years before I really learned about diversity of culture and race. In fact, it wasn't until I moved to South Florida when I became acutely aware of the conflicts that we struggle with due to our lack of respect for other cultures or knowing how to make room for one another. I'm still learning how to reach out in this area.

I also hadn't learned about urban concerns such as homelessness, crime, privacy, security, and mobility. Over the years, I've lived in or near Philadelphia; Atlanta; York, Pennsylvania; and Miami. Each area taught me more about reaching out to broaden my perception of what's around me and how to improve my ability to relate. I've also had the pleasure and honor of traveling abroad. I've been to Germany, Holland, France, Austria, Russia, Costa Rica, Jamaica, the Bahamas, Bermuda, and Italy just to name a few. What a wonderful joy and education each trip has been. The more I learn, the more I realize just how little I know. The more I reach out, the more I discover to reach out to. The more I relate with new people, places, cultures, and ideas, the more I grow and mature.

Where were you when I laid the foundation of the earth? Tell me, if you have understanding. Who determined its measurements—surely you know! Or who stretched the line upon it? On what were its bases sunk, or who laid its cornerstone when the morning stars sang together and all the heavenly beings shouted for joy? ... Can you lift up your voice to the clouds, so that a flood of waters may cover you? Can you send forth lightnings, so that they may go and say to you, "Here we are"? Who has put wisdom in the inward parts, or given understanding to the mind? Who has the wisdom to number the clouds? Or who can tilt the waterskins of the heavens, when the dust runs into a mass and the clods cling together? Can you hunt the prey for the lion, or satisfy the appetite of the young lions, when they crouch in their dens, or lie in wait in the covert? Who provides for the raven its prey, when its young ones cry to God, and wander about for lack of food?
Job 38:1–7, 34–41

Job had suffered beyond most of our ability to even comprehend. His friends had come to console, challenge, and be with him. They spent long hours debating the purpose of his suffering. They exhaustively argued with Job and one another. Finally, God speaks the above basically saying Enough! Who are you? Where were you? What do you know? And can you? We so easily get so full of ourselves. This world, creation, universe holds so much more for us to include in our care than we can ever begin to grasp. Regardless, we know that somehow we must relate with it all, somehow we must reach out and discover our place in its midst. Be clear that you do have a place, a purpose in the midst of the known and unknown. You are important. It's probably not a good idea, though, to play King of the Mountain with creation.

What Is It? was written by one of my favorite poets, Mary Oliver. What a beautiful expression of the awe of creation. "How could anyone believe that anything in this world is only what it appears to be?"

The frogs freeze into perfect five-fingered shadows,
but suddenly the flower has fire-colored eyes
and one of the shadows vanishes.

Clearly, now, the flower is a bird.

Have you taken the time to celebrate the awe of your surroundings? When I was in seminary, I would climb Stone Mountain and sit high up on a rock. I would go there because it was private and I could see nothing created by human hands. It was wonderfully holy ground for me. One day, during my meditations I heard a train go through the trees and could just make out its movement among them. That was the day that I remembered humanity with creation. I realized, for better or worse, anything we create becomes part of creation with us. For me to only enjoy the beauty of what I considered natural, was for me to reject and not respect the wonderful gift of co-creativity that God gave us and that we use, for better or for worse. A bird makes a nest, a bear uses a cave, a human builds a home. Reach out, learn, relate …

The more we open ourselves to the relational world around us, the more we begin to recognize and hopefully accept our responsibility to and with this world. Not everything is going to be pleasant or beautiful, but it does exist and we must figure out what our relationship to it is going to be. The bottom line question that I use in making absolutely any decision in my life is: What is the life-giving response here? Naturally, it sounds saintly. Trust me; there are plenty of people who will tell you of my lack of sainthood, me among them. However, asking this question helps me to focus on the most important issues and guides me into more helpful responses.

There's a terrific African adage: When the toe is stubbed, the eye cries. How simple yet profound. What happens on the other side of the earth does have an effect on us. Living in the Florida Keys, my neighbors and I have become quite knowledgeable about hurricanes and how to read their behavior. In fact, one of the first things I noticed was that by watching the African coast we are clued in to storm activity. This is even true for other things. One year there was dust from the desert in that part of the world that actually affected the Keys' atmosphere.

The health of our coral reef four miles off our shores has significant impact on fish life, thus professional fishermen, thus the fish market, thus the price of fish throughout our country, thus the economy, thus your pocketbook and diet, thus your stress and health. So the next time you come to visit our beautiful Florida Keys and are tempted to reach out and touch that incredibly beautiful reef, just that one light touch—don't do it! Human touch kills that part of the reef, which can then spread and often does. For the sake of all creation, never chip off a piece! Sometimes to reach out means to simply respect space and the right to be.

Hurricane Andrew had damaged a building that held a number of exotic snakes that were being studied. Among these were the Burmese pythons that you've probably heard have greatly multiplied and are eating our pets and indigenous animals. When the toe is stubbed, the eye cries. What you do in your yard, what you plant in your yard, what junk you toss into it, what chemicals you use or don't use, affects the people around you and much, much more. How you conduct yourself at work affects everyone around you.

I've been reading a book called The Power of Nice. The authors tell a story about how they were trying to capture the business of a major company. In anticipation of their final presentation, they worked diligently to produce a product they felt would be a real draw. The day came, the executives arrived and the presentation was made; then they sat waiting for the decision. The visiting executives started off by singing the praises of the doorman downstairs. This man had been remarkable in his kindness and thoughtfulness as he welcomed this group to the building. The executives told them that anyplace that had that kind of service at the door had to be the right place. The doorman won their account for them! All he did was be nice. When the toe is stubbed, the eye cries.

My community, the Florida Keys, is most definitely paradise. However, living in paradise comes with substantial trials. Unfortunately, a majority of our residents have reacted to those trials by using drugs and alcohol as a salve. Because I care about my neighbors, I've chosen to reach out in ways that will hopefully empower them to take control of their lives again. In recent years I've been learning about addictions and rehabilitation. This is a huge learning curve for me, and I don't know if I've built enough of a foundation to really make a difference, but I refuse to turn my back and ignore those things that are killing my community.

One of the interesting things I've learned is about how difficult it is for some people to reach out because they've become so withdrawn. One of the chaplains in charge of spiritual care at the Hanley Center in West Palm Beach shared one of his techniques for helping people move beyond themselves. He will take a person outside and have them sit down anywhere. Then he'll point out a rock or a branch or flower—anything really. He gives the person a paper and pencil and tells them to just sit and look at the object for ten minutes. After ten minutes, they are instructed to close their eyes and keeping their eyes closed to draw the object. The only way to be able to do this is to really focus on the object, to move beyond self and focus fully on the object.

I've thought about this exercise in relationship to things like the appalling oil spills or injustices committed against people. Would you be able to carelessly toss used car oil into the lot next door if you really valued your relationship with the people who live there? Would you be able to waste food by letting it rot in your refrigerator if your sister was homeless somewhere? In order for any artist to be able to draw so beautifully, they must have a deep value for whatever they are drawing. The very best cooks are the ones who cook from a deep appreciation for the food they are cooking and the people they are cooking for. The best friends are the ones who genuinely grasp and accept your faults as well as your beauty. In order for us to be the best we can be, we must reach out and be in relationship with all creation. Then we will recognize the value of life all around us; our worldview will become broader, more informed, and much fuller.

When we're in pain we tend to withdraw from the world even after we've gained a breathtaking appreciation for that same world. Grief, pain, loss, fear, vulnerability of any sort can take over our lives. When we build a foundation of reaching out and a wealth of love for the world we live in, intentionally reaching out during those difficult times of our lives becomes easier to do. We may need to, and probably will have to, really push ourselves to break out of our own skin, our own prison, but we will be much better equipped to reach out and heal.

ACTIVITY 5

1. Reflect on the beliefs that you were surrounded by when you were young. Write them down and consider how these beliefs affected you. Remember even those things that you discarded have had an effect on the development of your beliefs as they exist today.

2. Draw a picture; write a poem or prose to express how you see yourself relating to the rest of the world, and more, the rest of creation as of today.

3. What does the African adage, "When the toe is stubbed, the eye cries," mean to you? What does, "When there's violence anywhere, there's violence everywhere," mean to you? What does the plight of homeless people mean to you?

4. Where can you grow in your understanding of your relationship with creation? Choose one thing and make a plan to address that area.

CHAPTER SEVEN : MORAL MATURATION

My ethics students wrestle with the question: What is morality? What makes something moral? What is the relationship between morality and ethical conduct? Is morality a definitive construct or a multi dimensioned and varied viewpoint? And once you answer that one … says who? If something is moral for you does that mean it is moral for everyone? Why?

The basic question is: What is the right thing to do? In order to understand what it is that convinces you this is the right action to take, your next question must be: Why? The students initially think the answer is easy and quick. After we've spent a good thirty to forty-five minutes filling up the board with a massive number of things that influence morality, we've begun to learn. I don't believe it's possible for humans to put together a definitive list. Some of the things on my list include religion, faith, spirituality, family, friends, culture, rules, laws, experiences of all sorts, relationships, worldview, and much more. It's daunting to even try to figure out how to begin to unpack a portion of all that. Yet, if we are to responsibly understand and develop even our own morality, this is where we must begin.

How do you decide what is the right thing to do? What has influence on your decision?

When I was five years old, my aunt lived down the street from me. She had these wonderfully fragrant concord grapevines all over a frame covering the porch to her back door. Every time I would walk by Aunt B's home I would slow down, drinking in their rich fragrance. I could just imagine the amazing taste they would have. One day, I plucked a bunch off the vine as I quickly walked by the house. Hurrying to my home, I plopped down on the front porch swing; taking in their rich fragrance as I filled my little mouth with one great big succulent grape. Closing my eyes, I began to bite down in anticipation of the joy to come. My brother, Duffy, came around the corner, jumped up on the porch, grabbed my hand, and said, "Ohhhhhhh, you stole those grapes." Of course I responded with a resounding, "I did not!" as I choked on the monstrous one in my throat. "Aunt B did not say you could have them." "Yes, she did! Here taste one they're soooo good." Duffy then told me how the police were going to come and take me to jail. I began crying. He began singing, "I'm telling Mom, I'm telling Mom," as he darted around the house to get Mom to call the police.

Now I'm bawling, terrified of going to jail and angry with my brother for ratting on me. I sat sniffing and crying great big crocs as Mom came around the corner with the "rat." She was furious until she saw me. "I only ate one! I'll put them back." I whimpered through my choking, sniffing, and crying. Mom sat down and Duffy stood by, proud as a peacock. I don't remember what she said. She definitely was not happy with me but realized I had learned my lesson. My punishment was I had to go to Aunt B, tell her what I did, and apologize. I did, and Aunt B was gracious. At five years old I learned not to steal, confession is good for the soul, and that grace makes the world a much better place to live. Thinking back, I find it interesting that the lesson about stealing and confession took, but the lesson about grace … well, I seem to forget to share that one every so often, even now.

It's funny how slow we can be to learn some things and quick with others. Of course, what we learn and how well we learn directly affects our morality, our sense of right and wrong. Clearly my family has a significant place in the development of my morality. I wonder, if I had grown up in a homeless family, what would I have learned about stealing? Is it okay to take food from someone's garbage? Is it okay to take an extra cookie when only one was offered, so your brother can have one too? Is it okay to take a bunch of grapes to quench a deep thirst earned in the hot sun of a summer day? How does one define stealing? How do we decide what is the right thing to do?

I just watched the premier of a new television show called *Harry's Law*. The attorney was defending a young boy who had become addicted to drugs. The rehabilitation clinic where he had been working through recovery had closed and he was caught, for the third time, buying drugs. According to the third-strike law, the fact that he was a good boy caught up with a disease he had no way of controlling on his own and received no help didn't make the least bit of difference. That is, until his attorney spoke up for him in court. She told the truth, the hard truth, the one we don't want to hear. The truth that there are gray areas of life where grace can turn a life around and harsh judgment can destroy it. She appealed to the jury to choose to do the right thing, not necessarily the thing the law says but the right thing nonetheless. The jury chose harsh punishment; however, the judge chose grace. The boy was to be held accountable but in a way that gave him one more chance along with the support he needed to make success a real possibility.

Ahhh, yet another lesson … this one has been a surprise to every one of my ethics classes so far: the law is not necessarily ethical or moral. We follow the law, not because it tells us the right thing to do; we follow the law because it is the code of conduct that our society has decided upon. It is the code of conduct that we have agreed to follow regardless of our individual moral codes. Of course, we'd like to believe that ethics/morality comes into consideration in the process of determining the law, but the law is not about morality. It is simply about setting an agreed-upon code of conduct for a particular society.

For instance: The law says that marijuana is illegal. There are some people who have very strong opinions but have not yet developed a moral stance. Usually they have a difficult time when asked about their stance. They become quite agitated if someone disagrees with them. They usually will also make the "argument" quite personal either by feeling attacked themselves or by attacking the other person. On the other hand, some morally agree with this law because their moral beliefs are in line with this law. They tend to be more comfortable expressing their carefully examined viewpoint. There are also some people whose moral beliefs hold them in conflict with the law. Perhaps they believe that it is right to empower people to make their own decisions about what they introduce into their bodies. Perhaps they believe that marijuana has legitimate medicinal qualities for which there is no equal substitute, and the law takes away a person's right to this medicine. There are many reasons people develop their personal moral beliefs. Often, these beliefs are backed with a significant amount of passion.

As a child, I leaned on my parents, church family, and older brother to guide me in the right direction. However, as I got older I began to rebel so that I could stretch my wings. I wanted to explore my own individuality as any healthy teen will do. Fortunately, I had begun my personal relationship with my Creator years earlier. To date, there is no relationship that I value or trust more than this one. As a result of many experiences, I've learned that the One Who Loved Me into Being will never let me go, will never walk away, will never abandon me. This lively relationship has kept me from making some terrible choices during my teen years.

I must stress that the relationship that has been the most significant, the most trustworthy, and filled with complete fidelity on the part of the other is my relationship with my Creator. Please do not mistake this for the church or Church. The Church by any definition is not God and will never be God. The Church would have taught me that I could not be clergy even while it has always been the Triune God who has called and ordained me. The Church would have me believe that homosexuality is a sin. The C/church makes mistakes. As much as I love the church, it is not and never will be the Divine. It will make mistakes. Ecclesiastical fellowship and worship is a wonderful and necessary part of my growth in my relationship with the one who calls me beloved.

The church can be a valuable help guiding us as we develop our morality, but please be careful about letting it determine your morality for you. What you learn from the church must be weighed with all you've learned about the one who calls you to living in life-giving ways. Your relationship with this Embracer and Sustainer must always be central to all decision making. Everything else must serve to point you toward this center. If instead something points back to itself or somewhere other than to this one, leave it behind. It will not serve you well to keep it in your life.

Even though I grew up in the Pennsylvania Dutch country, drugs were a very real temptation in our school. There were several girls who just felt that I had to try drugs. They were relentless and vicious about it. Finally, they became so frustrated with me that they "captured" me in the girls' bathroom. With a few of them guarding the door outside, their leader and one or two others had me inside while the leader beat me up. This kind of pressure made me even more certain that illegal drugs or the more casual name for it, recreational drug use, was definitely something I wanted no part of. Clearly, using drugs in ways that they are not intended to be used has bad effects on the body and mind. I couldn't understand why I would want to do something harmful to this body that God gave me. My community had taught me that the best way to say thank you to God was to honor God. I could see no good that would come from using drugs in harmful ways.

I'm now fifty years old and have never used illegal drugs. The fact that I've been able to be successful in staying true to this as well as other moral choices gives me increasing strength to continue fidelity to my own self. I feel very strongly about my moral decision concerning the use of drugs and alcohol. My passion is based on my deep appreciation for everything my Creator has done for me. I honor God through my deep desire to show appreciation by taking care of my body in this way. Additionally, even as a child, I witnessed people destroying their bodies, lives, and relationships by using drugs/alcohol in harmful ways. I had every desire to learn from their mistakes.

In addition to my relationship with my Creator, my family and friends, and my faith community, my morality is further developed through dialogue with all kinds of people from all different cultures, backgrounds, and training. I've learned so much from my "Intro to

Ethics" students at the local college. It's amazing how much I learn when preparing to guide others. I'm convinced that as an educator, I actually learn more from my preparations and my students than my students could possibly learn from me. My students are required to team up and lead the rest of the class through a conversation on a specific ethical dilemma effecting current society. My students come from a wealth of countries, cultures, professional interests, and ages. They never cease to amaze me with their insights as well as their naïveté. Their courage is in measured and informed tackling of issues such as euthanasia, right to arms, abortion rights, equal rights, treatment of terrorists, and so much more, and their willingness to guide others in balanced yet passionate dialogue is encouraging. One of the most difficult things to learn is how to respectfully listen to opposing viewpoints with the purpose of understanding. The difference from the beginning of the semester to the end of the semester is truly astounding. Teaching these students has helped me to grow in my own ability to better understand and develop my own ethical stance, to listen to and encourage the expression of opposing viewpoints, and to stretch and challenge my own ethical choices.

I've discovered that the more I understand about what I believe and why, the more secure I feel; therefore, I am better equipped to listen to opposing viewpoints without anxiety. The only exception is that I have no interest in listening to another person's point of view if they demonstrate no interest in hearing mine. To me, conversation and dialogue is a two-way street. In fact, now I am truly fascinated by hearing opposing viewpoints and what it is that leads the individual to hold them. This becomes difficult if the individual is not willing to respond to questions. Often, by being able to truly listen for the purpose of understanding, I learn intriguing new things. One of the key things that I've learned, as I explore the world of ethics is that we have to be careful what questions we are asking. So often we are asking the wrong questions, and we end up not truly understanding the gravity of the situation we are faced with.

The book that I use for my ethics class, *Exploring Ethics,* which is edited by Steven M. Cahn, gives a perfect example of the importance of asking the right questions. In a chapter on cultural relativism by James Rachels, an example from the Eskimo culture is cited. In his discussion, he includes the fact that this small and isolated group of Eskimo settlements seemed to have very little regard for human life. Apparently, infanticide was quite common, especially with female babies. What's even more amazing is that there was no social stigma or punishment attached to this. They even extended this attitude toward their elderly. When someone became too frail to be useful, they were left out in the snow to die. Of course, most people are horrified at these revelations. Can you imagine living in a world where we would say that it's moral to kill babies and the elderly if you live in this culture but it is not moral in another culture? Yet, this is where the facts seem to lead us.

Rachels leads us to a deeper discussion of this situation. He reveals the reason, the answer to the "why?" question, concerning this particular behavior. By asking why, we discover the extreme harshness of the Eskimos' lifestyle. The Eskimos nurse their young into preschool ages, and a mother cannot always provide enough nourishment for all of the children. Additionally, there is the concern for transport of the babies. The mothers must carry the babies with them as they go about their daily work. Even with the help of additional family members, not all families are able to attend to the needs of all the children. Furthermore, the males are the primary food providers, the hunters. Hunters suffer a high rate of early death; therefore there is a high percentage of females to males.

The author goes on to discuss a number of reasons the Eskimos carry on this behavior. As a result, the reader comes to the realization that the assumption that Eskimos have an essentially low regard for human life is a horrible misinterpretation. What is really happening is that the Eskimos have realized that sometimes drastic measures must be taken in order for the society as a whole to survive. He also mentions that they do give as many children for adoption as they possibly can. They had needed to resort to these behaviors as a result of the culmination of life's hardships.

Therefore, the most effective question to ask is, What is the underlying reason for this behavior? When we ask that, we discover that the Eskimos are living out the same concern for society that we do. Society must continue to exist in order for us to exist. What is the greatest life-giving response to this issue? This is the question. Of course, as situations change, the answer to this question will also change.

So the questions you ask yourself are very important. First you must take an inventory of your personal history. What are the primary influences on your decision making? How have these things made a difference in your life? Have you been consistent? I'm amazed at how many people carry situational ethics with them. I can't tell you how many well-intentioned upstanding members of congregations that I've served have thrown personal attacks my way because of the hymns I choose for worship or my style of preaching, and at the same time they profess to be Christians.

How do you choose what is important enough to address? As I write this, there is grave political upheaval in the Middle East, economic instability throughout the United States, severe lack of appropriate health care options for over 50 percent of my local county—and our congregations are upset because they don't like praise songs, there's a woman in the pulpit, and someone's name was left off of the prayer listing. What is the state of your morality?

Pettiness has no place in the lives of those growing in their moral maturity. Life is way too short. If you are serious about your spiritual being, then you cannot allow the little differences of life to cause any strife in your life or living. Morality focuses on the important issues of spiritual living.

Recently two children were discovered in the back of a truck, lying among the discarded paraphernalia of insecticides. One child was dead and the other child not expected to survive. There are people who've been around these children in recent weeks who saw something was not right. Someone, in the recent past, shook their head mumbling about how some people just don't deserve to have children. They may have even mentioned to close friends about the terrible treatment these children were receiving. However, if asked why they didn't call it in to 1-800-96ABUSE, there would be a myriad of excuses. "Well, I don't have proof." (You don't need proof, just suspicion.) "That's not my responsibility." (According to Florida statutes *all* residents are required to report suspected abuse.) It's none of my business. (Really, the safety of children, the elderly, and the handicapped has nothing to do with you? You really believe that you are not called to love your neighbor as yourself?) "Well, if I'm wrong, then just look at the havoc that family will be put through." (Well, if you're right, just think of the lives you would save.) "DCF doesn't do a good job anyway. They can't be trusted." (If this is what you believe, then what are you doing to change that?)

I'm a member of a local organization that helps women and children live healthy lives. During one of our meetings, we were discussing fund-raising. Fund-raising is difficult in the best of circumstances, and here we are struggling with major economic strife, in the county with the highest cost of living in the state, lost jobs, and foreclosures, and short sales riddling our neighborhoods. Unfortunately, the majority of Monroe County residents deal with stress by abusing alcohol or drugs or both. The people at the meeting decided to have their fund-raisers at the local bars because that's how they could raise the most money.

I was stunned. How could this be? I stood up and expressed my concern. Each of the tables had posters that we were to be posting in our establishments warning that pregnancy and alcohol don't mix. I raised the concern of mixed messages. How could we possibly go to the bars to raise money for pregnant women? How could we possibly encourage drinking so we can increase our coffers? How could we possibly do this and then expect to be taken seriously when we discourage women and children from drinking? My concerns were met with dissention. No, let me clarify that: my concerns were met with downright anger.

The most distressing response for me came from a Christian lady sitting next to me. This lady was not only Christian but also holds a very high position in the community. She urged me to sit down and be quiet. She said, "They don't think like we do." If I've learned anything from a lifetime of working in churches and with domestic violence, it's that stopping the silence stops the violence. If we remain silent about the things that really matter, then we might as well have committed the crime itself.

My morality, my spirituality does not allow me to remain silent when it matters. This does not mean that I have to use fighting words or be antagonistic in any way. I simply must speak up, hopefully in ways that those I'm speaking to can hear what I'm saying. Remember to keep that which is most important at the forefront of your responses. The healthy lives of women and children matter. Respectable reputations being established so that we would be taken seriously in these situations matter. Speaking up when the lives of others are at stake matters. How do you decide what matters? How do you appropriately express what matters and when?

We cannot assume responsibility for how others hear us; however, we can hold ourselves accountable to how we communicate with others. While this is a different discussion than morality, it applies to a certain degree. If we do not assume responsibility for our own people skills, then how can we possibly expect anyone to respect anything that we have to say? If we are living spiritually then our relationship with others must matter to us enough to address our people skills.

When I was serving a congregation as director of program, I was beginning to try to understand my own struggle with people skills. I had such a good heart and deep faith; however, I was also intensely passionate about life. My energy level was extremely high. I moved fast, thought fast, talked fast. I knew what I was talking about and had some very good ideas; however, no one seemed interested in hearing them. I couldn't figure out why. One evening I attended an important dinner at the church. I sat with a family, and we had, what I thought, was a very interesting conversation. The one daughter was applying to colleges. What a wonderfully exciting time of anyone's life. I was quite interested in hearing her story and excitement. I asked her if she knew what she wanted to major in. She responded with an interest. As I asked her more about the subject area, her mother spoke up and reminded her of the importance of her decision. She told her daughter that if she made the wrong decision now, she would mess up her whole future. She went on to give examples of people who chose the wrong thing for their degree and then were never able to use it. This is wasted time and money.

Not meaning to cause any type of dissention or trouble, I shared that my bachelor's degree was in music education, yet as director of program I found my education to be very informative and helpful. I shared this information because I honestly thought it would be helpful. The next day, I was called into the senior pastor's office and reprimanded in front of the mother. She had come to the office to complain about my rudeness and inappropriate comments. At the time I was very confused by this. I tried to understand what I had done wrong. I tried to apologize to her and explain that I was honestly just participating in the discussion and didn't mean to be rude in any way. However, I was not allowed to speak even to apologize. I simply had to accept my reprimand.

Looking back, I now understand what the issue really was for this mother. While I completely disagree with how this whole thing was handled, I'm able to recognize that there were obviously family issues that I wasn't aware of. My focus on what I wanted to share blocked my ability to really hear what was going on among these family members. I was listening on the surface but not hearing the real meaning. As a result, my sharing was not heard as I intended, rather it was heard from the perspective from which this family was struggling with one another. The pastor didn't want to have to deal with any of it, so he just brushed it away to satisfy the squeaky wheel.

While I was not at fault for a large part of what happened, there was a lesson in it for me. The lesson was, if I'm going to respond to my calling to be a spiritual leader, then I must be ready to set aside my own needs when "on duty" and listen carefully to do my best to hear what the issues really are. By doing this, I have the best chance to address each situation from the most helpful perspective I possibly can. People don't always reveal what's really going on with themselves, but I must at least try to hear. On that day, during that dinner, I didn't even try. I simply joined in the conversation, not taking my responsibilities as seriously as I needed to.

Before we can make any difference, before we can expect anyone else to take us seriously, before we can begin to earn a person's respect and trust we must care enough about ourselves and others to listen carefully. We must continually develop our ability to hear from our spiritual centers. I'm convinced this is a lifelong area of growth. I'm also convinced that we must share grace and forgiveness with ourselves for our shortcomings, however major or minor. It's important to remember that God is not finished with me any more than God is finished with you.

Recognizing how our morality interfaces with other aspects of our spirituality is also of key importance. As you worked through the chapter on introspection, hopefully you reflected on who you are, what you stand for, and what has influenced your life and living. As you continue developing your morality, you'll discover that there are inconsistencies between your morality and who you are or what you believe. I know this is true because I'm reasonably certain that you, like me, are human. We are not perfect. I know it's a shock. Recognizing these dichotomies takes maturity and grace. Addressing them takes forgiveness and reconciliation.

Prior to the train wreck, I believed that when you are true to your faith, in good relationship with yourself, knowing who you are and what you're called to do, faithfully attending to that calling; you would also be in good relationship with others. Your characteristic behavior would be cooperative, happy, fulfilling, and supportive. I believed that to be defensive, rude, angry, and especially raging was completely out of character, inappropriate, and just plain wrong. If you were negative in this way then you couldn't possibly be in good relationship with the one who embraces you.

I struggled with this a few years after the train wreck. I had a terrible time reconciling my horrible behavior that I just couldn't seem to contain, control, or stop. Following is an excerpt of a prayer that I wrote out:

I'm so confused. To others I appear to be functioning very well; however, I'm struggling. Yes, since the train wreck, I've done truly amazing things. I'm alive, I walk, I provide spiritual leadership, I make a difference, I have become financially stable, I deal with the pain and am creating ways to continue, I'm working again and creating imaginative ways of providing spiritual leadership. But, I'm not serving as a pastor of a local congregation. What did God call me to? I always said spiritual leadership. I never felt that my calling was restricted to the local church. The problem is that the Church only considers pastoring a local congregation as the central passage for answering God's call in the ministry of Word, Sacrament, and Order. However, I have continually found that my ministry of Word, Sacrament, and Order is best carried out when I'm outside the walls of the "church."

My students find that my openness to the greater spiritual experiences beyond the language and restrictions of the institutional church empowers them to explore their faith. Halle halle halle! It's amazing how, when I help cultivate an atmosphere for the work of the Holy Spirit amidst the freely open explorations of humanity even on an individual basis, God, Lover, the one, Embracer, Mother, Father, Creator ... whatever language one might use to refer to this incredible creative divine love that continually brings life and new life, this embracer warms the heart of those in exploration blossoming beyond anyone's anticipation. Can the Church really deny the power of this unique form of Word, Sacrament, and Order?

In writing several months later, I was still struggling with this same theme, just in a different way:

What I feel today ...
Depressed and frustrated because I don't know why and can't stop feeling this way.
Lonely and not sure why, because I have friends, many friends, who really do care about me.
Anxious and frustrated because sometimes I lose my temper, mainly when I feel threatened. Why can't I just wait a few seconds, think, and put it into perspective?
I've also noticed that I can't get myself to take time and think and then respond even in playing games. I have a desperate need to resolve everything instantaneously. The more I try to get myself to slow down, the more anxious I get.
I can't get myself to do anything.
I want to cry and am having a hard time being patient with myself about it.

I was confident and very active in my relationship with my Creator; however, I was also unbelievably angry, even in rage. I simply could not reconcile this dichotomy. My psychologist assured me, this was most definitely a result of the PTSD that I was struggling to live with. However; even though I know my PTSD is chronic, as in permanent, it seems that I had imposed a time limit on myself. Deep down, I told myself that it was time to be over it. I had no right to still have any temper issues. I was embarrassed that I had not been able to work through the oceans of anger and rage by this point. I was thankful for the progress that I had made, but still could not give myself any brownie points. I believed that I should be over it by now. I'd been angry too long.

It's not that I wasn't working on my issues. It's not even that I wasn't progressing. It also was not due to any lack of faith or any lack of relationship with God. This all had been happening because I was and am determined to continue to heal. I refuse to be a victim to Amtrak's mismanagement any longer. The thing that was causing this whole struggle and self-judgment was a true lack of understanding of the insidious nature of PTSD. PTSD involves a chemical imbalance in the brain. My hypothalamus had been violently rattled back and forth. On top of all this, because my pain level has been so extreme and initially they were not able to fully diagnose what was causing my horrific level of pain, they had me on two different kinds of morphine and valium every day for three years. Narcotics also have a detrimental effect on the brain, especially when used for extended periods of time. I couldn't understand that it simply was not possible for me to control that which was out of control due to trauma, brain injury, and chemical imbalance. My doctors kept encouraging me on. They kept assuring me that I was improving; that the injuries were just so severe that healing would take time and there were some things that I would have to deal with for the rest of my life.

I was slowly beginning to learn that there are some things outside of my control that were affecting my behavior. Bootstrap theology (which is pulling yourself up by your bootstraps) has no place in reality. I now have a much greater understanding of people who appear to be just plain angry and rude all the time. We never know what might be going on with that other person. Sure, it's possible that they simply have little or no relationship with God. However, there could easily be other reasons. It's possible that they have a deep abiding relationship with the Divine that is pulling them through despite the pressures society puts on them.

This understanding helped me to become more forgiving and patient with myself. I learned to let people know about my PTSD and to apologize quickly. Most people were accepting of my explanation and have allowed me the space I need. The doctors were correct—with additional time and continual TLC given to myself, I've been able to heal to the point that my anxiety levels are generally at a level I can handle. I also am aware of my boundaries. So when those boundaries are being approached, I am equipped with tools that keep me from going off the deep end most often.

I now realize that my inconsistencies with my own characteristics and moral character are not always simply a matter of pulling myself up by my bootstraps, and that's okay. Recognizing the intricacies and sometimes surprising twists and turns my own personhood takes helps me to share the life-giving grace with others that was so difficult for me to learn to share with myself.

Developing our own morality involves a tremendous amount of self-reflection, patience, honesty, work, forgiveness, and willingness to learn and grow. Sometimes you'll find yourself learning an old lesson all over again yet in a deeper way. Consistency and integrity are vital to this process. If you are a systematic person, then you might want to draw up a plan for your own moral development that includes goals and objectives. If you are more of a pragmatic or practical person, you might prefer to address your morality as life presents various moral issues. Either way, you'll need to be intentionally aware of what is going on around you as well as within yourself. You might find a spiritual director to be helpful to you in this process.

Activity 6

1. Find a place where you are able to reflect without interruption, perhaps in a park, by a waterfall, at the beach, or in a closet—whatever works for you. Equip yourself with something to write or draw or paint on. Begin an inventory of those things that have contributed to your moral code over the years. Once you have the

inventory, organize the items. Perhaps some things had influence at one time but not another. Reflect on what caused that change. Was it a good change? What were the foundational influences? Were they positive or negative?

2. What are the current things influencing your moral code? Where is your relationship with God in the system of your morality? Are there changes that need to be made? Are there shifts that need to be made?

3. Develop a plan to move your morality into a healthier place. Make sure the center of your code is the one who calls you beloved.

CHAPTER EIGHT : PERSONAL RELATING WITH A HIGHER POWER

There was a huge painting in the sanctuary of my church when I was six and seven years old. I used to just stand there and study the painting. It was so curious to me, because I couldn't imagine where the person who painted it got the idea. The reason I couldn't imagine was because it just didn't ring true with my experience. When I asked the adults about it, they would tell me with absolute confidence that yep, this was what God looked like. They were telling me that God was a heavy old man with a super long beard, sitting on this throne that was covered up by his enormous robe that filled even the very corners of the painting. The eyes had depth in them with what I considered to be wisdom. However, the painting exuded domination and judgment, and demonstrated no room for me. At least, that was the message that I was getting from this painting. One day a lady at the church shared her joyous interpretation of the painting with me. For weeks after that, I would stand in that room, alone with the painting, trying to get her interpretation—and I just couldn't. To me, this painting had no resemblance whatsoever to the God that I had experienced.

Remembering all this now, I realize how amazing it was that, somehow, to me God wasn't so much who or what others told me, as much as God was the one that I experienced. I certainly didn't have a romantic impression, because in addition to the gracious, loving, nurturing, feeling God, I also knew the God who allows children to die horrible deaths. I didn't understand this dichotomy at the time, I just knew it was. I knew that God allowed my brother to die the way he did. I also knew that God's tears washed over me that day in the sanctuary. In fact, while this contradiction is more understandable to me today, I certainly can't say that I really comprehend it even now. The important point here is that my understanding as well as lack of understanding is all based on our relationship. The more I take time to focus on relating with my Creator, the more our relationship grows.

This is not to say that recognizing and accepting these ambiguities is not important. My intent is to stress the importance of allowing haziness to exist in your relationship with the one who loved you into being. C .S. Lewis beautifully portrays this aspect of our relationship with God in his collection, The Chronicles of Narnia. In book 2 of the series, The Lion, the Witch and the Wardrobe, Aslan is a lion who Lewis created to represent Jesus Christ. A group of children develop a relationship with Aslan, who surprises them with his amazing compassion and gentleness. At a point when they experience him as ferocious and terrifying, he reminds the children that he is "not a tame lion," since, despite his gentle and loving nature, he is powerful and can be dangerous.

One of my favorite sermon titles is "Jesus Was Not Nice." Generally, people are shocked to hear this. We have so romanticized Jesus that we have muted his divine voice. He wasn't being "nice" when he cleared the Temple of the money changers. In the American society, we so often uphold people who "smooth things over," people who "never have a cross word," people who are "gentle." While there is certainly a time and place for these characteristics, there is also a time and place for truth telling, accountability, honesty, and sometimes even sternness. We don't have to be mean in this process, but it's often important to clearly communicate boundaries even if it's not considered the popular thing to do. Jesus the Christ, God, our Redeemer, the one who provides for our salvation often surprises us, maybe even offends us. God doesn't always tell us, lead us, affirm us, nurture us in the way we think God should. God is not always nice.

I recently watched an astonishing movie called God on Trial. It's about Jews in Auschwitz who actually held a tribunal to determine whether or not God had broken his covenant with the Jewish people. They go through all the arguments that you and I struggle with when faced with much less: Is it that God is not good just with us? Is it that we broke the covenant through free will and this is our punishment? Does God use evil people to accomplish God's purposes? Is our suffering a sacrifice for the greater good? Is it not for us to know the mind of God? If God is so confusing and unknown to us, how are we to know how to relate with God?

It's so easy for us to just turn our backs on such a confusing and "unseen" God. When we come across a confusing human that challenges us too much, we just walk away. Why wouldn't we do the same to a God who is not only confusing but difficult to see? I'm hoping you are jumping up and down with all kinds of arguments right now. But just in case you are saying, Yes, finally, someone with the guts to voice my thoughts, I want to encourage you that this was part of what our Jewish brothers were struggling with in the trial while at Auschwitz. To struggle with this question and much more is human.

I'm convinced that God has no fear or anger over these honest struggles. I'm convinced because when I sat under that table screaming at God, the divine held me in my Creator's right hand and baptized me with life-giving tears feeding me with the communion of wholeness and healing. I'm convinced because when Job sat in mourning with his friends and demanded answers from God, he received God's life-giving presence and divine response. I'm convinced because after all we humans have done; God still abides among us, calling us to choose the right paths. We've given our Creator, Redeemer, and Holy Spirit every reason to smite us, yet here we are still bumbling along, and we are not alone.

I must assume that there's something that's made you seriously consider, if not believe, that God is there. What is it that leads you to this belief? Take some time to write your thoughts down, maybe even share them with someone else. Where have you experienced God in your life? Do you believe simply because others that you trust told you that you should? If so, start to look around you and begin to name the evidence.

I'm blessed to live in a place where I can watch the sun rise and set over the water. These are stunningly beautiful. Science has been able to explain the beautiful colors of these experiences as well as the timing, locations, and much more. To me, that makes the wonder of this amazing creation all that much greater. How is it that all of this could possibly exist by chance? Additionally, how boundless the intelligence must be that brought it all into being.

Talk to God, talk to creation expressing your awe. Tell the dog who owns you how amazing she is. However, I wouldn't advise doing this too often as they do get rather full of themselves. Did you ever notice how they respond? How could that be? What is intelligence? Celebrate the wonderment of it all. Live in the unknown for a while. Admire that which is greater than you. Spend a day, a week, all of your life in amazement. I even talk to my trees and garden. My favorite is my mango tree. My mango tree symbolizes hope, life, and the symbiotic relationship between me and the rest of creation. I was in a wheelchair when I personally dug the hole in the cap rock and planted this amazing tree. The trunk has an interesting curve in it because when it was young a hurricane provided significant challenge to its survival. I've planted, watered, fertilized, trimmed, and nurtured this wonderful tree over the years. In return, it has brought me great joy, beauty, tasty nutritious mangos. To the bees it has given nectar, to the birds a safe haven, to my neighbors yummy fruit, to all of us oxygen … there is no end to the many blessings.

I'm convinced these blessings are all gifts from the one who gave and gives and will continue to give life and blessings to all of creation out of gracious αγαπε, love. As a result, I can do nothing less than converse with my mango tree through the language of love, nurturance, and yes even spoken language. I believe my Creator delights in this exchange.

In the midst of my unknowing, daily, in fact minute by minute, I go to God in so many ways. I remember when I was in first through twelfth grade, throughout the day sitting at my desk, practicing with the band, especially walking through the hallways I would talk with God. I'd say a little prayer here and another one there. I simply understood God as my constant companion. Sometimes my prayers would be formal, other times it would be in the form of simply talking with my ever-present intimate friend. I never understood the complaint that someone was trying to take prayer out of the schools. It's simply not possible, not when children talk with God as their constant companion. I wasn't always asking for things; sometimes I was merely looking for God's presence. Actually, I thought this was something everyone did. It never occurred to me that people didn't know God so intimately.

Today I do the same thing. However, I have added something else. Now I set aside special times for me to simply be quiet and listen. My favorite place to do this is in my hammock in the backyard. I'm so blessed with my home, which I share with my wonder dog, Sweetie. Our backyard is private and surrounded by trees; it is always breezy and has wonderful shade. My neighbors, friends, and family have become quite accustomed to seeing me in the hammock. Sometimes, Sweetie joins me, sitting on my belly sleeping. I lie there, looking up through the mixture of Poinciana, Gumbo limbo, and sea grape branches and leaves at the sky. I watch the clouds, birds, stars, sun, and moon. I listen to the breeze, the fountain of water, and the birds. I listen deeply for God's wisdom revealed in so many ways. I wait.

Letting go of myself and my thoughts is the most difficult part of listening. Have you ever thought about how you listen to other people? What's going on inside your head as you "listen"? Are you planning supper, planning what to say, thinking about what you don't agree with, daydreaming … where is your "head" at when you listen? If you're like most people, you'll realize that you're doing just about anything but truly listening to hear what the other is saying. Quieting our minds and egos takes practice. If we don't practice, we will never really hear anything or anyone. We are not listening if we are thinking, "What are they saying?" We are listening when we hear what they're saying. In order to hear, we must get outside of ourselves and into the meaning of our current speaking companion.

We are hearing when we ask questions for clarification. We are not listening or hearing when we ask questions to make a point. In order to hear, we must open ourselves to the vulnerability of listening from within the sphere of the one speaking. We must love enough to set aside our bias for the moment and open ourselves to experience the bias of our companion as best we are able.

When I was in seminary, one of our professors took it upon herself to guide all her students toward a life of meditation. She specializes in church history and has been deeply moved by the Mothers and Fathers of the Desert. Dr. Roberta Bondi became a dear friend of mine during seminary. She has written many books that would be wonderful guides for your journey. One day, my colleagues and I were discussing our struggles with prayer and daily meditation. Dr. Bondi's open understanding and acceptance of our struggles was quite a relief.

As clergy, we are often expected to be completely comfortable in our communications with God. However, we struggle with the ups and downs of life just as anyone else. Sometimes, in the midst of our daily struggles, our communication with God becomes strained. Someone asked her how much time she spends, each day, in meditation with the Creator. Her response was overwhelming for many of us. Fortunately, she followed up with encouragement to start with what we would feel comfortable with on a regular basis: one minute, five minutes, and thirty minutes. She gave us permission, which opened the door for us. We trusted that as we became comfortable in our time with God, we would naturally increase our time. I've found this to be very true.

I use a variety of materials in my regular meditations with the Source of All Being. My favorite was written by another friend of mine: Sacred Journeys: A Woman's Book of Daily Prayer written by Jan L. Richardson. This treasure guides you through the entire liturgical year giving the reader calendar dates to correspond. Jan uses stories of women she has encountered through her own journey and invites the one in meditation to travel along the way. A resource recommended to me by Roberta is: The New Companion to the Breviary with Seasonal Supplement. This companion has morning, daytime, and evening meditation guides that take you through the liturgical year as well as the calendar of feasts and commemorations. Readings, responses, traditional canticles, and prayers are included. I have also used some of Roberta's books in my meditations. Among them are my favorites: To Pray and to Love and To Love as God Loves . These books engage the reader into deeper spirituality through the writings of early monastic writers. I found them to be exhilarating. As I journeyed through each book, the differences in language and culture coupled with the gracious guiding explanations by Roberta led me to explore my own faith, my own spirituality, my own communication with God with renewed eyes and heart.

The labyrinth has also provided a remarkable space for me to pray, listen, and hear. The first time I used this spiritual tool was at the annual conference for the Florida United Methodist Church. I'd been struggling with a very difficult decision for several years. In the past, I'd taken my difficulties to God through prayer, tears, anger, and pleading. It had come to the point where I had to decide; should I stay in the marriage or move on. My husband was and still is a good man, but he was in a downward spiral that seemed to have no good end in sight. I had tried everything I knew to do and not to do. I was coming to the realization that being married to me was pushing him further down the spiral, I had become an enabler. This horrific realization is what I took to God that week as I walked the labyrinth over and over and over. As I walked, I simply talked to God and cried and tried to listen.

My first steps were quite uncomfortable. I was embarking on something I had never experienced before. There were so many who expressed significant hostility toward the labyrinth. I wasn't sure if it would be something helpful to me or not. However, I was absolutely certain there was absolutely nothing evil about it. Walking the path was actually more difficult than I expected. While there is only one path from the outside to the center and back, somehow I found myself missing a step from time to time and repeating a few patterns. As I became absorbed in the path, I chuckled at my clumsiness. I realized that I would still get to the center; it just might take me longer and be a bit more complicated than was supposed to be. I realized this as I stepped outside the labyrinth without having ever been to the center. I stood dumbfounded.

As I looked to the center and longed to get to my center, the reflection occurred to me about how similar my life experience was to my experience with the labyrinth. Starting again, I began reflecting on the many twists and turns, how sometimes I would be getting closer to the center and in the next moment how far away I'd be. I held a small clamshell reminding myself of my baptism. First I thought of my baptism with my father and older brother, Duffy, who died in that Labor Day accident a few months after our baptism. Then I thought of my baptism by God's tears that day in the sanctuary. I thought of my husband's baptism. I thought of God's love for both of us. My soul stretched trying to hear, to understand, to receive the divine life-giving breath, breathing life into me.

The labyrinth is an ancient meditation tool. Dr. Lauren Artress has written a number of books on the history and use of labyrinths for insight, healing, and deepening spirituality. Dr. Artress says, "*All of the larger-than-life questions about our presence here on earth and what gifts we have to offer are spiritual questions. To seek answers to these questions is to seek a sacred path.*" She relates how labyrinths have been used as sacred paths by almost every religion. In her book, Walking a Sacred Path, she also discusses the mystery connected to labyrinths as well as their four-thousand-plus years of history. She brings to light their geometric ambiguity. The wonderful insights discovered by using the labyrinth are celebrated throughout her writing.

Having read Dr. Artress's writings ahead of time, I was thrilled to have an opportunity to explore the gifts of this sacred tool. By the end of my weeklong spiritual journey on the labyrinth, I felt confident that I had arrived at the most life-giving decision. I had to go home and end something I had truly intended to be for life. However, in the ending was to be a new beginning, a fresh new life for each of us. Now, more than ten years later, as very close friends we both look back and thank God for the divine blessings that came with this decision.

As I've continued to deepen my relationship and conversation with God, I've come to the exciting revelation that the One Who

Loved Me into Being is so much greater than I will ever be able to define, describe, or understand. This eye-opener has led me to the place where I cannot justify using "God" as a name for this Divine Giver of Life. In fact, I cannot justify naming at all. Naming is a very powerful thing. Naming someone gives us a certain control that I can't possibly claim. This is why I use such a variety of describers: Creator, Triune God, One Who Loved Me into Being, Holy Spirit, Guide, Lover, Mother, Father, Redeemer, Divine Giver of Life, and so many more. These describers are how I am able to center myself on the particular divine presence or gifts that I'm focusing on in the moment. I still use the reference "God" because the majority of society does use it as the name for the Trinity, and that's how I was raised.

I begin my conversations with one or several describers and then I simply talk. As I write this, I'm most focused on Giver of Life. I'm sitting in my hammock, listening to the birds, water, distant traffic, watching the leaves of the traveling palm, pink lady, fiddlewood, and other tropical plants sway in the gentle breeze, enjoying the wafting scent of fiddlewood, key lime, and kumquat blossoms gently flowing around me. I'm enjoying the shade of the eighty-year-old trees around me as I say: "You've given so much life, it's just surrounding me and yet here I am a part of it. How do you do that? How is it that you can love so completely that life just springs forth? Thanks. Thank you so much. Do you ever get to just sit and enjoy like I do? Thank you for these moments of peace and belonging, for these moments of assurance yet mystery."

And then my mind wanders to remember the children in homes and towns and countries of violence, and I say, "Please help them to know you're with them. Please show me how to share your love with them appropriately. Please guide me and others, Lord. Amen." This is just a very brief and unplanned moment of conversation with my Creator. Brief, but it fills me with so much wonder, awe, and fullness that it carries me through the day. I'll have many more brief conversations yet today. These conversations are largely unplanned but incredibly intimate. They are deeply treasured moments of my life that I couldn't imagine living without.

What I hope you recognize is that God, the one to whom you pray, hears all prayers. There is no particular language that must be used. In fact, when I was recovering from the train wreck, there were times when I wasn't able to speak complete sentences—I couldn't even think in complete sentences. I can't tell you how frustrating it was to have thoughts, needs, and fears, and not be able to call for help or share. I realized that even though I couldn't think in conversational ways, I was able to perceive what I wanted to communicate. Deep in my soul I went to the Giver of Life with my perceptions, and I knew I was heard. I knew I wasn't alone and that parts of me that even I didn't understand were understood and being cared for. I settled into the folds of God's right hand, which was upholding me. God "knows" you and me.

So far, I've only talked about our conversation with God. But there are always at least two participants in conversation. Just as with any person, when we're in conversation with God we must silence ourselves and listen. Listening is something most of us don't do well. Even when listening to the Divine, we often have so much going on inside our heads and hearts that we don't actually hear. As hard as it is to truly hear another person, it's even harder to hear God. At least with other people there is an audible voice. With God, we must listen with all our senses as well as our inner being. Once again, I must urge you to read Roberta Bondi's To Pray and to Love. Roberta's realistic and compassionate writings on prayer cannot be matched.

While with my colleagues in Dr. Bondi's classes, we revealed that one of our greatest struggles was learning how to discern the voice or word or guidance of the One Who Loved Us into Being. It's like when you're with someone who shares that she loves blue roses. Do you hear her say she loves blue roses, or are you hearing her say that she wants some blue roses? How do you discern her meaning? You could ask her; however, if she is someone who is too shy to be honest, she might deny her true meaning. So you must learn her style, her tendencies, and her character. And sometimes you simply don't know unless she reveals the truth to you.

Discerning your Creator's meaning isn't any easier. Sorry. I know you were hoping that I had some magical formula so you could always be absolutely certain of all the divine leadings in your life. There are many Christians who claim to be absolutely certain of God's meaning and exactly how to bring it to fruition. They will tell you that if you are truly a Christian and in close relationship with God, you will know exactly what you are to do. These Christians always have a hard time with me. I believe it's because I honestly believe in creative chaos. I truly am just as convinced that the supreme experience of God, our greatest spiritual growth, comes when we allow ourselves to struggle through the dichotomies of our living. I cannot claim to infallibly know the leadings of God. However, in the process of growing my relationship with the Divine, I gain clarification to some level of understanding. So often, it's like the person who values continually furthering their education. It seems that the more you know, the more you know that you don't know, and that's oddly comforting.

The longer we work on our relationship with the Divine, the more we learn about ourselves, the Divine, and interestingly enough, others. The more we love God, the more we love ourselves and others. The closer we get to our Creator, the closer we are to ourselves and others. The spiritual work we do can only improve our lives and living. This relating with the Giver of Life is by no means simply an intellectual affair. Our emotions are deeply intertwined in our spiritual journey.

Emotions are yet another divine gift, a blessing. Life is so full of ups and downs and each person is so unique that we often become overwhelmed with emotions; if not their strength, simply their diversity. There are some cultures that relish the expression of emotion and others that relish the silent experience of emotion. Regardless, everyone has emotion, experiences it, and expresses it one way or the other.

Interestingly we even have feelings about our emotions. Some are embarrassed by emotions, seeming to think that there is something inherently wrong with both the feeling of them as well as the expression of them. In the Pennsylvania Dutch community where I grew up, we felt that we were quite expressive of our emotions. However, having lived in a great variety of other cultures, I've learned that people often perceive us as being quite stoic. Of course, as I reflect on the emotive expressions of some of these other cultures, I find myself shocked and often overwhelmed by their behavior. One isn't right and the other wrong. Humanity has developed a great variety of ways to explore this dynamic divine gift.

My community is incredibly musically gifted. We sing, play instruments, dance, and write music. Our musical expression is superb, as we understand music as yet another divine gift that empowers us to express the depths of our beings otherwise unrevealed. However, to many cultures we appear stoic while at the same time producing incredible music. To many this is a great mystery. How can they stand so still and look so solemn and actually be feeling anything? Yet, the music is flawlessly expressive and beautiful. I've directed many church choirs. Oddly enough, these choirs have been quite culturally diverse but primarily Caucasian. If I had a penny for every time I said to my choirs after singing something like "He Lives!", "Okay, great, now let's sing it again and how about we smile and look happy about it this time." Generally the choir will chuckle, realizing their demeanors, begin to sing again and actually have to struggle to smile. Usually they are not able to smile and actually physically express joy throughout the hymn. It's not that they're not happy. In fact, it's the opposite. Many of us have been taught that to express appropriate reverence in the midst of this divinely inspired joy, we must be solemn. Yes, it sounds counterintuitive, and in fact it is; but it's also true for some cultures.

Meanwhile other cultures believe that unrestrained expression of emotion must be present in order for true worship to have happened. I've preached in congregations that actually had ladies equipped with handkerchiefs waiting in the aisles for those who became overwhelmed with the spirit or emotion during the service. To these congregations, appropriate reverence in the midst of divinely inspired joy must be met with dancing and shouting and whooping.

Emotions are a divine gift bestowed upon humans. Emotions are not evil or wrong or good or bad; they simply are. They are divine blessings that empower us to experience the ups and downs of living and the diverse character of creation. Without emotions we would have no way of responding to interpersonal relations other than fight or flight. I don't know about you, but that certainly doesn't sound like fun to me. We are empowered to respond to all aspects of life and living in ways that give meaning to the colors of the sunset, give depth to a kiss, significance to an accomplishment, and greater worth to living. We honor the one who gifted us with our emotions by using our gift in life-giving ways.

The absolute best way for me to express my emotions is through music. My Creator blessed me with this incredible gift of cocreating through the amazing gift of sound, breath, rhythm, numbers, emotion, body, material, connection, mystery, and movement all beautifully weaved together and exquisitely delivered as music. What an incredibly creative gift. I remember when I was eight years old and just beginning on my plastic recorder, I had no idea that music was going to become such a life-empowering and life-giving companion. I was just beginning to discover what would become my most treasured communication with the one who gifted me in the first place.

At first it was just learning notes, position, breathing, and tonguing. I cherished the joy of being able to play simple melodies. After time, I began to realize that the notes and rhythms I was playing had an effect on my feelings. I began to experiment with playing these simple songs with a variety of emotions. This was when I began to understand the true value of phrasing, dynamics, vibrato, tonguing styles, and so much more. But it was when I began to open myself up to conversing with God through music that I discovered the value of the soul, the deepest most complete part of myself in music. When I play, there's something that comes from deep within that is otherwise untouchable. It feels like communing with creation. Music has become my most treasured communication with my Triune God. Breath is vital to all musical expression. I'm fully aware of the ruah (breath of God) the Holy Spirit's empowering action throughout my playing. I never feel more complete than I do when playing. There is a freedom and joy unleashed, and I get to share it with everyone willing to hear.

Often, in the evenings, I'll lay in my hammock watching the stars and moon. I've always wanted to be able to travel through the universe. As I lie there dreaming, I wonder what the music of the universe sounds like. There must be sound, regardless of whether it can be heard by human ears. Recently, my boyfriend was helping me learn about the deaf culture. Both of his parents were deaf and most of his relatives are also. He shared a story about how his cousin had asked his hearing sister what sound her suntan made. At first, I thought this was a rather odd thing to ask. But as I thought about it, she was right on the mark. She figured the sun must make noise because it's so big and powerful. She's correct, the sun does make noise—we just can't hear it. I don't know if it's due to the distance or the limitations of our hearing, at any rate the sun does make noise. In fact, anything that involves friction makes noise. So I would imagine that the sun turning our skin a different color probably has some type of a noise to it also. We simply can't hear it. In the same way, the spinning, burning, revolving spheres of the universe must also create sound of some sort. To me, this unknown sound of the universe is its music. While my ears cannot hear it, my heart can. I imagine the Creator of all that is savors the harmonies of creation. I take great joy in joining my harmonies with this song of life. St. Francis of Assisi shares in this through his "Canticle of the Sun":

> *Most high, all powerful, all good Lord!*
> *All praise is yours, all glory, all honor, and all blessing.*
> *To you, alone, Most High, do they belong.*
> *No mortal lips are worthy to pronounce your name.*
> *Be praised, my Lord, through all your creatures,*
> *especially through my lord Brother Sun,*
> *who brings the day; and you give light through him.*
> *And he is beautiful and radiant in all his splendor!*
> *Of you, Most High, he bears the likeness.*
> *Be praised, my Lord, through Sister Moon and the stars;*
> *in the heavens you have made them bright, precious and beautiful.*
> *Be praised, my Lord, through Brothers Wind and Air,*
> *and clouds and storms, and all the weather,*
> *through which you give your creatures sustenance.*
> *Be praised, My Lord, through Sister Water;*
> *she is very useful, and humble, and precious, and pure.*
> *Be praised, my Lord, through Brother Fire,*

through whom you brighten the night.
He is beautiful and cheerful, and powerful and strong.
Be praised, my Lord, through our sister Mother Earth,
who feeds us and rules us,
and produces various fruits with colored flowers and herbs.
Be praised, my Lord, through those who forgive for love of you;
through those who endure sickness and trial.
Happy those who endure in peace,
for by you, Most High, they will be crowned.
Be praised, my Lord, through our Sister Bodily Death,
from whose embrace no living person can escape.
Woe to those who die in mortal sin!
Happy those she finds doing your most holy will.
The second death can do no harm to them.
Praise and bless my Lord, and give thanks,
and serve him with great humility."

Relating with my Creator is the single most important thing of my life and living. I might be focusing on my moral beliefs; however, I can only do this in response to my relationship with the divinity that created me in the first place. I cannot consider the right thing to do aside from my relationship with God. I cannot have compassion for miners trapped in Chile separate from my bond with the Giver of Grace. I cannot reach out, opening myself up to vulnerability without my liaison with the Healer. I cannot live my life without or aside from my relationship with the One Who Loved Me into Being. I cannot become who I am intended to be if I am separate from the Great I AM. Spirituality is the single most important thing of my life and living.

ACTIVITY 7

1. Take a few moments to reflect on ways that you would like to relate and communicate with God. What has worked for you? What hasn't?

2. Think about those things that haven't worked for you in the past. Why didn't they work? Did you expect too much of yourself, too fast? Did your schedule interfere? Were you uncomfortable

expecting family/friends to respect your time? Recognize what the challenges were in the past and plan ahead this time so you can find a way to work around them.

3. Visit a labyrinth and talk with someone at the location about their experience of the labyrinth. You could ask the pastor of the location to guide you for your first time there.

4. Listen to music of various types that honors God. Mozart, J. S. Bach, Petra, Sweet Honey in the Rock, Gaither, Wesley, Ruth Duck, Sylvia Dunstan, and many more. Fill your library with samples of the music that best expresses your love for God; then light a candle, turn the lights out, close the door, open the window, and listen to it.

5. What are the characteristics of your higher power: judgmental, gracious, mysterious, present, and comforting? Are these characteristics ones that you've adopted because of what others have told you or out of your own experience?

6. Set aside one or two minutes of complete privacy. Prepare yourself ahead of time to be ready to open your mind and listen, not think. Set a timer so you don't even have to think about the time. Close your eyes and hear. Don't think about what you hear, just open your mind to your higher power, God, Creator. After the timer goes off, you might feel like you didn't hear anything. That's okay. Give yourself a chance. Don't expect to hear anything in particular. Your heart will know. Do this for seven days. Perhaps just before your listening time or just afterward, you would like to take a minute or two to share your joys and concerns with the One Who Loved You into Being. You might like to light a candle, hold something sacred to you, and spread a cloth over your shoulders or on the floor. Do whatever helps you to set aside this minute as something sacred. You also might like to add a resource such as a finger labyrinth or a book of devotions to your special time with your Creator. Do all this slowly. Start out very simple and only add as you feel compelled to do so.

7. After a month of these sacred daily minutes, reflect on the characteristics of your Creator that you've experienced to date. Compare to your first list. Chances are that you will have greater experiences of God and will be aware of additional characteristics.

☐

CHAPTER NINE : CONTINUING THE PROCESS

Becoming the person you are intended to be takes a lifetime. Every one of us has the opportunity to continue developing; we just need to make the choice. Hopefully, this book has encouraged you to continue becoming not just today but for the rest of your life.

There will be dry spells as well as times full of life and growth. As long as you are truly focused on developing yourself to the best you can be, these dry spells do not need to be of great concern. You'll pull yourself out of them at the right time because your interest in your relationship with your Creator can do no less. The very nature of creation, Creator, cocreation demands continual change, growth, new life, renewed life.

The dormant times of creation don't necessarily mean that nothing is going on. Perhaps you need some time to process and even celebrate the growth you've just experienced. My 101-year-old grandfather was just telling my mom about the crocus that peeked out of four inches of snow. These wonderful flowers do that every year. There will be no sign of life from them for months. The ground will be frozen, slushy, frozen again, and buried under feet of snow for months. Then suddenly, when you think there couldn't possibly be any chance of life, up they bloom again. The crocus has been a sign of hope, joy and spring for generations of people. Your spiritual life can be much like the crocus but even better. While the crocus reemerges year after year after year, it remains the same. As your spiritual life resurges time after time, your being will continue to grow and blossom in ways you never dreamt were possible.

I've found that the most fervent times of growth have been the most difficult and painful times of my life. However, this does not happen spontaneously. Some of my most passionate and honest communications with God have been during these times. As a result of my sincerity and desperation I've been able to reflect deeper, hear more openly, and struggle through the difficulty in ways that have led me to reap amazing blessings. The catch is, in order to do this I have to push. I have to care enough about myself to fight for me in constructive ways. I can't just throw my hands up and play victim. I must choose to stand up, express myself clearly and fully to both myself and the one who brings life, breath, and salvation. I also must choose to listen and to hear. This is the most difficult part. Discerning the Divine Voice of Life versus my own voice or the voice of the status quo is not as easy as some make it sound. For me, the true test is to honestly ask the question: What is the most life-giving response for all involved? I always discern as best I can; however, I don't know that I can ever say that I truly get it right. In spite of this, I can honestly say that I do the very best I can and remain humble enough to make alterations as needed.

Continuing to grow spiritually requires focus; determination; love of God, self, and others; and humility. Learning how to love myself and be humble at the same time has been a tricky road for me. For many years I struggled with low self-esteem, continually beating myself up and never giving myself the credit or love I deserved. Low self-esteem is not the same thing as humility. Similarly, selfishness is not the same as loving oneself. Most of us struggle with the balance necessary during our lifetimes. Regardless of which direction you find yourself tipping the scale, it's the balance of love and humility for ourselves that is so important. Our love for our Creator and our neighbor is directly affected by how we respond to ourselves. In fact, the balance must include our love for all three. The health of our spirituality depends on it.

There will also be times where you will be amazed at the growth you are making or have made. These will be times when your focus on your spirituality will come to fruition through your life and living. You'll feel complete and fulfilled. Joy will permeate everything you do. These are wonderfully happy times when you will find that your life's work, family relationships, friends, and recreation all seem to be buzzing with life. Even when difficult or painful things happen during these times, you'll find that you'll be able to work through them in much healthier ways. Your emotions will not plummet or soar unrealistically. People will especially enjoy being around you. You will experience blessings in ways that will encourage you to celebrate your relationship with your God in ever growing and deepening ways.

I wish you the greatest joys in your future. Mary Oliver wrote a beautiful poem about becoming the best person you can and carrying that person into the world with you always. I believe this light that she speaks of is the light that gives life to living, the light of God shining through your living and blessing mine. The poem is called "The Buddha's Last Instruction."

"Make of yourself a light,"
Said the Buddha, before he died. ...
Slowly, beneath the branches, he raised his head.
He looked into the faces of that frightened crowd.

Try not to be frightened in your spiritual journey. You are not alone; your God remains with you even when you turn away. The One Who Loved You into Being also Loves You into Eternity.

May you always know the blessings of God through all things.
The Rev. Dr. Pamela Feeser

GLOSSARY

C/church

Traditionally, a small *c* is used when referring to church in general: i.e., I go to church on Sunday. A capital *C* is used when referring to the Church universal or as part of the name of a particular congregation: i.e., The Church has many denominations within it. In this writing, most references are to the institutional Church or universal Church; therefore, the *C* is, in most cases, capitalized.

Ecclesiology

This is the study of church. When we talk about someone's ecclesiology, we are talking about their understanding of what church is or means.

God

I use a number of descriptors for God. I prefer not to name God. Naming is a powerful tool that gives the one who names some authority over the one being named. I cannot feel that I have the right to any authority over the One Who Loved Me into Being; therefore, I cannot be so bold as to name my Gracious Nurturing Redeeming Ever-Present Embracer. Instead, I choose to invoke the Divine by using descriptors of the characteristics that I've experienced throughout our relationship.

Labyrinth

A labyrinth is different than a maze. In a maze, you run into dead ends and have to backtrack. A labyrinth has only one path, and it leads you to the center and then back out again. This path will have many twists and turns, sometimes closer to the center and sometimes further away. An excellent resource for learning about labyrinths was written by Dr. Lauren Artress: *Walking a Sacred Path: Rediscovering the Sacred Labyrinth.*

BIBLIOGRAPHY

Alexander, Hartley Burr. *Native American Mythology*. Mineola, NY: Dover Publications, Inc., 2005.

Artress, Dr. Lauren. *Walking a Sacred Path: Rediscovering the Labyrinth*. Riverhead Trade, 1996.

Augsburger, David. *Caring Enough to Confront: How to understand and express your deepest feelings toward others*. Ventura, CA: Regal Books, 1973.

Blenkinsopp, Joseph. *Interpretation: A Bible Commentary for Teaching and Preaching*. Vol. Ezekiel. Louisville, KY: John Knox Press, 1990.

Bondi, Roberta C. *To Love as God Loves:Conversations With the Early Church*. Philadelphia: Fortress Press, 1987.

—. *To Pray & to Love: Conversations on Prayer with the Early Church*. Minneapolis: Fortress Press, 1991.

Carter, E. Russell. *The Gift is Rich*. New York, NY: The Friendship Press, 1955.

—. *The Gift is Rich*. New York, NY: Friendship Press, 1979.

Committee, The UM Book of Worship, ed. *The United Methodist Book of Worship*. Nashville: The United Methodist Publishing House, 1992.

Covey, Steven. *7 Habits of Highly Effective People*. Free Press, 2004.

God on Trial. Directed by Andy DeEmmony. 2008.

Ernest Kurtz and Katherine Ketcham. *The Spirituality of Imperfection: Storytelling and the Journey to Wholeness*. New York: Bantam Books, 1992.

Friedman, Edwin H. *Generation to Generation: Family Process in Church and Synagogue*. New York: The Guilford Press, 1985.

Hay, Julie. "Cycles of Development." *Family Issues*, 2003: 1-16.

Holy Bible: New Revised Standard Version. Division of Christian Education of the National Council of Churches of Christ in the United States of America., 1989.

Lewis, C.S. *The Chronicles of Narnia*. Vol. 2. 7 vols. New York: HarperCollins, 1978.

Linda Kaplan Thayler; Robin Koval. *The Power of Nice: How to Conquer the Business World with Kindness*. Broadway Buisiness, 2006.

McBride, J. LeBron. *Spiritual Crisis: Surviving Trauma to the Soul*. Binghamton: the Haworth Press.

Mello, Anthony de. *One Minute Wisdom*. New York: Doubleday-Image, 1988.

Moore, Thomas. *Care of the Soul*. New York: Harper Collins, 1992.

Oliver, Mary. *House of Light*. Boston: Beacon Press, 1990.

Richardson, Jan L. *Sacred Journeys: A Woman's Book of Daily Prayer*. Nashville: Upper Room Books, 1995.

Smith, Huston. *The World's Religions*. San Francisco: Harper, 1991.

Tan, Amy. *The Joy Luck Club*. New York: Penguin, 2006.

Taylor, David L Bartlett and Barbara Brown, ed. *Feasting on the Word*. Vols. Year B, Volumn 4. 12 vols. Louisville; KY: John Knox Press, 2009.

the Carmelites of Indianapolis. *The New Companion to the Breviary with Seasonal Suppliment*. Indianapolis: Camelite Monastery, 1988.

The Rev. Pamela Feeser, D.Min. *Buying the Vineyard: Different Options for Living, Playing, and Hoping in Non-violence and Safety: DOLPHINS*. Miami, FL: Dissertation for doctoral work at South Florida Center for Theological Studies, 2003.

Young, Wm. Paul. *The Shack: Where Tragedy Confronts Eternity*. Los Angeles, CA: Windblown Media, 2007.

ABOUT THE AUTHOR

Pamela Ann Feeser grew up in the Pennsylvania Dutch community of Hanover, Pennsylvania. Choosing to honor her Creator by working toward perfecting the glorious gift of music given to her, she began her professional life studying music at West Chester University. With her BS in Music Education, she continued on as a school musician educator and director of music in the church as well as a performer. Following a move to Central Florida, Dr. Feeser heard her call into the Ordained Ministry. She chose to respond to this call by completing her Master of Divinity degree at Candler School of Theology at Emory University and was ordained by the Florida Conference of the United Methodist Church in 1994. In 2003 she earned her Doctor of Ministry degree through Florida Center for Theological Studies focusing on proactive ministry in domestic violence. Her music, and educator and pastoral skills all combine to empower her ministry to this day.

Dr. Feeser currently ministers through Living Springs Counseling, a DBA of DOLPHINS to Stop Domestic Violence, Inc. Dr. Feeser is the founder and executive director of DOLPHINS where she works as a Certified Pastoral Counselor. In addition to training community leaders equipping them to help prevent domestic violence by addressing issues from their role in the community, she provides pastoral counseling, couples counseling, workshops and assists her underserved community in affording prescriptions and recovering from Hurricane Irma. In addition, Dr. Feeser has taught religion and ethics classes at various local colleges.

Dr. Feeser lives in Key Largo, Florida, where she feels blessed to be able to celebrate life each and every day.
Her website is http://DOLPHINSLivingSprings.com.

May you always know God's Blessings through all things.

-Pam Feeser